GRAND CANYON

• THE COMPLETE GUIDE •

2nd Edition

WINNER
(1st Edition)

Benjamin Franklin Award
Best Full-color Travel Guide

Independent Publisher Book Award
Best Travel Guide

JAMES KAISER

CONTENTS

THE SOUTH RIM (p.106)

The most famous and popular part of Grand Canyon. Home to nearly two dozen easily accessible viewpoints. Stay at a historic lodge, dine on a gourmet meal, or simply take in the breathtaking views.

THE NORTH RIM (p.244)

Wild and remote, the North Rim combines gorgeous scenery with one-tenth the crowds of the South Rim. Because of its cool, high elevation, the North Rim is covered in alpine forests of spruce, fir and aspen, giving it a feel more like the Rockies than the desert Southwest.

COLORADO RIVER (p.196)

Often referred to as the Nile of America, the Colorado flows free for 277 miles in Grand Canyon. Along the way it passes through a stunning landscape hidden from much of the outside world. Without question, a river trip through Grand Canyon is one of the most fantastic adventures on the planet.

HAVASU FALLS (p.298)

Part tropical paradise, part Southwestern dreamscape. Remote Havasu Canyon is home to two of the most beautiful waterfalls in North America. The only challenge is getting there.

OVERVIEW

ONE MILE DEEP. Ten miles wide. One hundred sixty miles long. Covering 1.2 million acres in northern Arizona, Grand Canyon is a breathtaking act of geology. Teddy Roosevelt called it, "the one great sight every American should see." The panorama from the rim is one of the most impressive sights in the world, but Grand Canyon is much more than just a pretty view. Hidden within its depths are fascinating creatures, geologic marvels, the ruins of an ancient civilization, and some of the best outdoor adventures in North America.

Cut by the Colorado River over the past 5 million years, Grand Canyon is a colossal labyrinth of towering buttes and deep side canyons. Although massive, most visitors head to one of two developed areas: the South Rim or the North Rim. The South Rim, located two hours north of Phoenix, is by far the more accessible and popular of the two. Home to six of the park's eight lodges, it's what most people think of when they think of Grand Canyon. The North Rim is located just south of the Arizona/Utah border, one of the least densely populated places in America. Its remote location means fewer crowds—with equally stunning views.

Hiking trails descend from both rims to the bottom of the Canyon. Along the way they pass though 11 layers of ancient rocks, ranging in age from 250 million to 2 *billion* years old—nearly half the age of the earth. At the bottom of the Canyon, near the junction of three popular trails, lies Phantom Ranch, an overnight lodge offering comfortable beds and home-cooked meals. Guided mule rides along the trails are also offered.

Twisting through the bottom of the Canyon is the Colorado River. Fed by Rocky Mountain snowmelt and passing through America's great deserts, the Colorado is the most impressive river in the West. Although currently plugged by dams along much of its length, the Colorado flows free in Grand Canyon, dropping 2,000 feet in 277 miles. Each year, roughly 20,000 people embark on guided river trips through Grand Canyon. In addition to 60 thrilling rapids, river trips provide access to spectacular hiking trails, stunning Indian ruins, and gorgeous waterfalls. Without question, a river trip through Grand Canyon is one of the most incredible outdoor adventures in the world.

HIKING

GRAND CANYON OFFERS some of the best hiking in America. The range of scenery in the park is incredible, from cool pine forests to narrow slot canyons to everything else in between. There are trails that skirt the edge of the rim and trails that plunge thousands of feet to the Colorado River. And don't forget the canyon's 2 billion years of amazing geology—arranged chronologically for your viewing pleasure.

Sound too good to be true? Not at all. But before you hit the trail there are some important things you need to know. First, there are two types of hikes in Grand Canyon: day hikes and backcountry (overnight) hikes. Day hikes are very straightforward—just pick a hike and go. No special permits are required. Backcountry hikes, on the other hand, require a bit more planning. Due to the overwhelming number of visitors who want to go backcountry hiking each year, the National Park Service limits the total number of backcountry hikers allowed on each trail. Backcountry hikers must apply for permits ahead of time, which are granted on a first-come, first-served basis.

Unlike most hikes on the planet, trails in Grand Canyon start at the top and end at the bottom. This "mountain-in-reverse" style of hiking leads to some unique challenges. For one, a hike into the canyon seems deceptively easy on the way down. Each year park rangers rescue hundreds of hikers who overestimate their hiking ability and become stranded near the bottom of the canyon. Remember that it takes about twice as long to hike up as it takes to hike down. Another factor to consider is the temperature; the lower you go, the hotter it gets, with temperatures up to 20°F hotter at the bottom of the canyon. Despite these challenges, hiking in Grand Canyon is an experience not to be missed. Just follow the rules and tips on the following pages and your trip will be safe and unforgettable.

If you're still unsure about hiking in Grand Canyon on your own, the Grand Canyon Field Institute offers a variety of first-rate backpacks, day hikes, and rim walks. This private organization, which works in partnership with the National Park Service, is dedicated to enhancing the understanding and enjoyment of the Grand Canyon through firsthand experience. Their activities accommodate a wide range of ages and experience levels. All are highly recommended. For more information call 866-471-4435 or visit www.grandcanyon.org/fieldinstitute.

DAY HIKES

There are two types of day hikes in Grand Canyon: day hikes along the rim and day hikes that descend partway down the canyon along inner canyon trails. The North Rim has the most day hikes along the rim, with about half a dozen popular trails. The South Rim only has one day hike along the rim: the Rim Trail (p.117), which passes by many of the South Rim's most popular viewpoints. Day hikes that descend into the canyon follow longer trails that start from both rims, and hikers turn around before reaching the bottom. If you plan on day hiking into the Canyon, give yourself plenty of time to return before sundown.

BACKCOUNTRY HIKES

If you're thirsting for more than a quick day hike, the park offers a number of spectacular backcountry hikes that start at the rim and drop down into the Canyon. These hikes, which are best tackled over multiple days, are called backcountry hikes because they follow trails that pass through terrain classified by the park as "Backcountry." The park service has divided the backcountry into four management zones: Corridor, Threshold, Primitive, and Wild.

Corridor Zone trails are well maintained and equipped with modern facilities. There are only three Corridor trails in Grand Canyon: the Bright Angel Trail (p.170), South Kaibab Trail (p.178), and North Kaibab Trail (p.280). Not surprisingly, these trails are the most popular backcountry hikes in the park. Because Corridor Zone trails are heavily trafficked and provide relatively easy access to water, Backcountry Rangers strongly recommend that first-time Grand Canyon backcountry hikers stick to Corridor Zone trails.

The **Threshold Zone** offers trails that are unmaintained but generally in fair condition. There are two Threshold trails covered in this book: the Hermit Trail (p.184) and the Grandview Trail (p.190).

The final two management zones, **Primitive** and **Wild**, cover extremely rugged terrain beyond the abilities of most Grand Canyon visitors. The Thunder River Trail (p.288) is the only Primitive Zone trail covered in this book. Considerable Grand Canyon hiking experience is necessary in Primitive and Wild zones.

To camp in the Backcountry, you must apply for a permit from the park Backcountry Office. Be aware that the backcountry is divided into "Use Areas" delineated on commercial maps. Knowing which Use Area a trail traverses is necessary when applying for a backcountry permit. Note that camping in the Corridor, Hermit, Monument, Horseshoe Mesa, and Tapeats Use Areas is limited to designated campsites or campgrounds, and camping there is limited to two nights per hike. (From Nov. 15 to Feb. 28, however, you can camp up to four nights in popular corridor campgrounds.)

BACKCOUNTRY PERMITS

Because the National Park Service limits the number of visitors allowed to camp in the backcountry, permits are required for all backcountry hikes. Each year, the park service receives about 30,000 requests for about 13,000 available permits. Although these numbers seem intimidating, if you plan in advance a permit isn't too hard to come by. On short notice, however, getting your hands on a backcountry permit can be an exercise in futility, especially in the summer months.

Backcountry permits are issued by the Backcountry Reservation Office. The earliest a permit can be requested is on the first day of the month, four months prior to the proposed start date. (For example, if you want to apply for a permit sometime in June—June1, June 15, June 30, etc.—the earliest you can apply is February 1.) Permit requests can be submitted via mail or fax, but are considered late if not received at least three weeks prior to the proposed start date. The back-country permit request form is available on the Grand Canyon's web site. Permit requests are processed in the order they are received. All written requests are responded to via U.S. Mail (allow at least three weeks for processing).

Although most people request permits well ahead of time, cancellations sometimes make same-day permits available. You can place yourself on a waiting list for same-day permits if you arrive at the Backcountry Information Center by 8 a.m. on the day you would like to hike. For detailed information on the back-country permit process, visit **www.nps.gov/grca/backcountry** or call **928-638-7875** Monday–Friday, 1 p.m.–5 p.m.

The South Rim Backcountry Office is located to the east of Maswik Lodge, next to the railroad tracks. Mailing address:

Grand Canyon National Park
Backcountry Information Center
PO Box 129
Grand Canyon, AZ 86023
Fax: 928-638-2125

FEES

There is a non-refundable $10 fee per permit, plus $5 per person per night below the rim, $5 per group above the rim. Permit cancellations are subject to a $10 cancellation fee. Frequent hikers may wish to purchase a one-year Frequent Hiker membership for $25 that waives the initial $10 fee for each permit. If a permit is cancelled three days or more before the start date, the $5 per person fee can be applied to a future hike.

HIKING TIPS

Don't hike from the rim to the river and back in a single day

Each year the park service rescues hundreds of day hikers stranded in the canyon. Hiking to the river and back seems deceptively easy on the way down, and by the time a weary hiker realizes how difficult the hike back up will be, it's often too late. On top of the added hassle for both hikers and park rangers, evacuations can be extremely expensive for the person evacuated. (A helicopter evacuation can cost upward of $3,000 per flight.) By planning ahead and understanding the trail, you can easily avoid a needless evacuation.

Bring plenty of water

The biggest dangers on the trail are not scorpions, rattlesnakes, or mountain lions (in fact, these animals pose relatively little threat), but dehydration, heat exhaustion, and heat stroke. In the sweltering summer months this danger becomes even more pronounced. Temperatures rise as you descend into the canyon. The average temperature difference between the river and the rim is more than 20°F. The best way to stay safe is to avoid hiking during the middle of the day and to drink plenty of water. Rangers recommend drinking a gallon a day in the summer. Drink small amounts often, even when you don't feel thirsty. (By the time you feel thirsty you're already dehydrated.) Although some trails have access to water, many do not. Make sure you're aware of water availability on a trail before you start hiking.

Bring plenty of food

Just as important as drinking is eating. Salty snacks replace electrolytes (salts) that the body loses through sweating. If you drink water but do not replace electrolytes, you run the risk of developing hyponatremia that can lead to seizures and death. Eat much more than you usually do, and eat small amounts often. Every time you drink, you should also eat.

Take regular breaks

Not only will this give you a chance to enjoy the fine views, it will make you a more efficient hiker. Resting for five to seven minutes can remove up to 30 percent of the waste products that build up in your legs while hiking.

Use common sense

Don't take shortcuts, don't approach wild animals, and don't engage in reckless behavior. By using common sense and taking a few moments to consider your actions, your Grand Canyon experience will be that much more enjoyable.

HIKING IN THE SUMMER

Not only is summer is the busiest hiking season in Grand Canyon, it's also the hottest time of the year. Summer temperatures frequently top 110°F on many Grand Canyon trails, posing significant risks to hikers including:

HEAT EXHAUSTION: the result of dehydration due to intense sweating.

HEAT STROKE: a life-threatening condition caused when the body's heat-regulating mechanisms become overwhelmed. Symptoms include flushed face, dry skin, weak and rapid pulse, high body temperature, poor judgment, and unconsciousness. Heatstroke victims must be cooled immediately—move the victim to shade and continuously pour water on the victim's head and torso.

HYPONATREMIA: The result of low sodium in the blood caused by drinking too much water, not eating enough salty foods, and losing salt through sweating. Early symptoms mimic those of heat exhaustion.

With careful planning, the dangers above can be avoided. One of the easiest preventative measures is to avoid hiking in the middle of the day when temperature are at their highest. Instead, hike in the early morning and late afternoon. By resting in the shade during the middle of the day, you will limit your exposure to the scorching rays of the sun. While hiking, a good way to stay cool is to keep your clothing wet. A wet T-shirt, hat or bandana around your neck will work wonders to cool you down.

DRINKING WATER

You should always bring your own water when hiking, but water sources are sometimes available on Grand Canyon trails. The Backcountry Office maintains a list of seasonal water sources and updates the list based on the reports of rangers and hikers. Piped water is seasonally available on the Bright Angel and North Kaibab Trails, and does not need to be treated. Water taken from creeks, springs, or the Colorado River should always be treated and purified. Water can be treated and purified in one of three ways:

- Filtering: Filter the water through a 1-micron filter, available at outdoor stores.
- Disinfecting: Use two drops of bleach or five drops of tincture of iodine per gallon of water. Allow the water to sit for 30 minutes before drinking.
- Boiling: Water should be boiled for one minute, plus one additional minute for every 1,000 feet above sea level.

The park service recommends filtering first, then adding chemicals. Hikers can also cache water on a trail for the hike out. Try to place cached water in the shade, and mark it with your name and expected retrieval date.

HIKING HAZARDS

Lightning

Lightning storms can sweep through the Grand Canyon at a moment's notice, especially in the summer. If you find yourself caught in a lightning storm, head to a low-lying area away from cliff edges, lone trees, or metal objects. Do not seek shelter in an area that could be subject to flash floods. While shallow overhangs may offer protection from rain, they will not offer protection from lightning and should be avoided.

Rockfalls

Rockfalls are most common during and after downpours. It is especially important to watch and listen for rockfalls during this time. Do not stand at places where rocks have obviously fallen before.

Snakes

Although the Grand Canyon is home to a variety of snakes (some of which are poisonous) snakebites are rare, occurring almost exclusively to people attempting to handle snakes. Be aware of where you place your hands and feet, and if you do encounter a snake, leave it alone. If you are bitten, contact a ranger or send someone for help.

Scorpions

Scorpions are common in the Grand Canyon, but they are rarely seen. Although a scorpion sting is painful, it rarely causes serious health problems. The elderly and young children are the most susceptible to scorpion venom. Hikers should always shake out their boots and clothing before putting them on. Campers should always check their sleeping bags and avoid walking around barefoot in the campsite. Having a flashlight in hand after dark is also a good idea.

Other Animals

Most other wildlife in the park is harmless, and those animals that could be potentially dangerous (such as mountain lions) generally stay away from people.

Flash Floods

Each year, flash floods kill about 200 people in the United States. The best course of action to avoid a flash flood is to avoid areas that are subject to flooding—such as stream beds, narrow canyons, and washes—especially during downpours. If you hear or see a flood coming, move to higher ground immediately. Do not try to outrun a flash flood.

FLASH FLOODS & DEBRIS FLOWS

FLASH FLOODS ARE one of the region's greatest dangers. Although dry for much of the year, heavy rains pound Grand Canyon in late summer. During monsoon season (July, August and early September) thunderstorms sweep through the region on an almost daily basis, sometimes dumping several inches of rain in a few short hours. The rocky, sun-baked landscape and sparse vegetation does little to absorb the water or slow it down, and the runoff from these storms is channeled into side canyons, some of which drain enormous areas. If the rain is heavy enough and the side canyon drains a large enough area, a wall of water several feet high can race through the side canyon at speeds topping 23 feet *per second*. The force of this flood is so powerful that it compresses the air in front of it, sending pebbles and small rocks flying through the air in advance of the approaching wall of water.

What is most frightening about flash floods is that they can form when skies are clear and sunny overhead. Storms in the region tend to be highly localized, dumping several inches of rain over a concentrated area while land a few miles distant receives none. In the late summer of 1997, 12 tourists were hiking through Antelope Canyon (not far from Grand Canyon) when a thunderstorm 10 miles upstream dumped an inch and a half of rain in less than an hour. The runoff from this storm gathered with astonishing speed, sending an 11-foot wall of water roaring through Antelope Canyon. The flood killed all but one of the hikers, who had been pressed against the canyon wall as the flood raged past. By the time the water subsided, every article of clothing on his body except his boots had been ripped off by the gritty, sediment-laden water.

Similar to flash floods, but even more destructive, are debris flows. Unlike flash floods, which are 80–90 percent water, debris flows are a deadly slurry of water, rocks and debris—up to 60 percent solid material by volume. They scream through side canyons at a maximum speed of 25 feet per second—three feet per second *faster* than flash floods—ripping out trees and sweeping away boulders that weigh hundreds of tons. Few people have ever witnessed a debris flow, but they create a deafening roar that shakes the ground. On average, two debris flows are triggered in the Grand Canyon each year.

MULE TRIPS

FOR OVER A century, mule rides have been one of Grand Canyon's most popular activities. Everyone from Teddy Roosevelt to The Brady Bunch has descended the canyon on mule, and while hardcore hikers would never dream of passing up a chance to hike into the canyon, for many people mules are the only way to go. These sure-footed animals are fun, convenient, and offer a genuine taste of the Old West. (And did we mention they do most of the hard work for you?)

Although less demanding than hiking, mule riding is still a physical activity. Riders must sit up straight on a moving animal for extended periods of time, which requires more endurance than you might think. And then there's the fear factor. Mules are incredibly safe animals, but they often walk terrifyingly close to the edge of the trail. (Sometimes it seems like they're doing this intentionally just to taunt you with their amazing sense of balance.) Mule riding is not for the faint of heart. But despite some mild challenges, few people have any serious problems riding mules, and most people consider the experience to be great fun.

The South Rim offers both day and overnight mule rides. Day rides head down the Bright Angel Trail (p.170) to Plateau Point (p.176) and arrive back in Grand Canyon Village by mid-afternoon. Overnight rides follow the Bright Angel Trail down to the bottom of the Canyon where riders spend the night at Phantom Ranch, a small lodge offering beds and home-cooked meals (p.115). Riders return the next morning via the South Kaibab Trail (p.178). Two-night rides are also available from mid-November through March. Reservations for South Rim mule trips are accepted up to a year in advance and are highly recommended for the busy summer months. The North Rim only offers day rides, including rides along the rim and rides that descend partway down the North Kaibab Trail (p.280).

No experience is necessary for a mule ride, but riders must be at least 4 feet 7 inches tall (1.38 m), weigh less than 200 pounds (91 kg), and speak fluent English so the mule can understand commands.

South Rim Mule Trips: p.119
North Rim Mule Trips: p.252

COLORADO RIVER TRIPS

A RIVER TRIP through Grand Canyon is one of the most incredible outdoor adventures in North America. Period. From fighting off frothing rapids to hiking up lush side canyons to reach hidden waterfalls, a Grand Canyon river trip is an experience you'll remember for the rest of your life.

Fifteen commercial outfitters are licensed to offer guided river trips through Grand Canyon. Trips range in length from one day to three weeks, and generally cost $200–$300 per person per day (longer trips are cheaper per person per day). The best trips are the multi-day adventures run between Lees Ferry (river mile 0) and Diamond Creek (river mile 226). (One- to three-day "sampler" trips run at the end of the Canyon can't compare with the scenery found in the heart of the park.) Some companies also offer trips geared to specific interests such as hiking, photography or natural history. Note: due to the immense popularity of river trips and the limited number of passengers the national park service allows on the river each year, many trips are often booked up to a year in advance.

Commercial outfitters run trips with both motorized and non-motorized boats. Motorized boats speed through the canyon at a fast pace, allowing you to visit more sights in less time. While some people find this convenient, others regret missing out on much of the inner Canyon.

Non-motorized boats come in two types: inflatable rafts and dories. Inflatable rafts cushion the impact of the rapids, making for a smoother ride through the Canyon. Dories, piloted by skilled boatmen, offer a more tumultuous ride where flipping, though rare, is a possibility. But for thrill seekers and river purists, these elegant boats are the only way to go.

River-running season in Grand Canyon generally lasts from mid-April through early November. Summer is the busiest time, but it's probably the worst time to go due to the heavy crowds and scorching temperatures. The best time to take a river trip is in the spring or the fall, when temperatures are mild and the river is much less crowded. Private, noncommercial river trips are also allowed, but the waiting time for a permit can last several years.

For more on running the Colorado River through Grand Canyon, see the Colorado River chapter on page 196.

RIVER OUTFITTERS

Aramark-Wilderness River Adventures
(800-992-8022, www.riveradventures.com)

Arizona Raft Adventures
(800-786-7238 www.azraft.com)

Arizona River Runners
(800-477-7238, www.raftarizona.com)

Canyon Explorations/Expeditions
(800-654-0723, www.canyonexplorations.com)

Canyoneers
(800-525-0924, www.canyoneers.com)

Colorado River and Trail Expeditions
(800-253-7328, www.crateinc.com)

Diamond River Adventures
(800-343-3121, www.diamondriver.com)

Grand Canyon Discovery, Inc
(800-786-7238, www.grandcanyondiscovery.com)

Grand Canyon Expeditions Company
(800-544-2691, www.gcex.com)

Hatch River Expeditions
(800-433-8966, www.hatchriverexpeditions.com)

Moki Mac River Expeditions
(800-284-7280, www.mokimac.com)

O.A.R.S./Grand Canyon Dories
(800-346-6277, www.oars.com)

Outdoors Unlimited
(800-637-7238, www.outdoorsunlimited.com)

Tour West
(800-453-9107, www.twriver.com)

Western River Expeditions
(800-453-7450, www.westernriver.com)

CHOOSE YOUR WEAPON

OAR-POWERED RAFT

Oar-powered rafts offer a great mix of safety and excitement. Their flexibility allows them to bounce off obstacles undamaged and absorb much of a rapid's energy, resulting in a much smoother ride. Tipping is rarely a problem, but expect to get wet. Some commercial outfitters allow passengers to help paddle rafts.

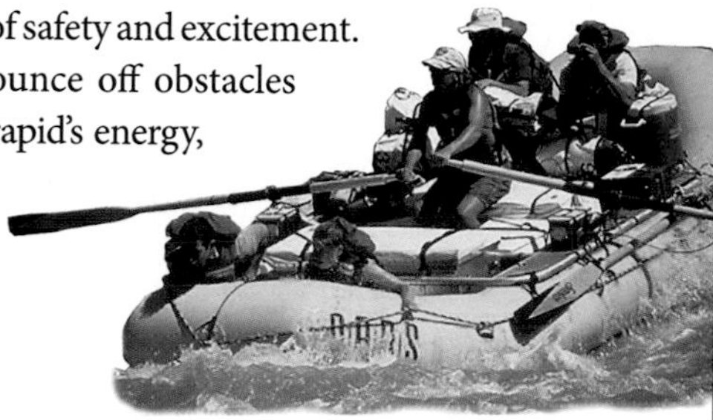

DORY

These wooden or fiberglass boats require the most skill to maneuver and are only paddled by guides. Because they ride like a roller coaster through the rapids (and occasionally flip over) dories are not for the timid. But they provide the most rugged, exciting and elegant ride Grand Canyon has to offer.

MOTORIZED J-RIG

J-Rigs are the biggest, most stable craft on the Colorado. Because they accommodate up to 20 people, they transport the majority of commercial passengers in Grand Canyon. J-Rigs speed through the Canyon faster than non-motorized boats, which can be a good or a bad thing, depending on your preference.

Photo courtesy O.A.R.S

SCENIC FLIGHTS

NO MATTER HOW much time you've spent peeking over Grand Canyon's rim, nothing can prepare you for the perspective you'll gain from the air. Viewed from above, the canyon's labyrinth of temples and buttes stretches all the way to the horizon. The sheer magnitude of the landscape and the incredible power of erosion are revealed in a manner hard to imagine from the ground.

More than 100,000 scenic flights soar over Grand Canyon each year. The best flights depart from Grand Canyon Airport in Tusayan, Arizona (just south of the main entrance to the South Rim). Both airplane and helicopter flights are offered, the main difference being the speed and elevation at which they fly. (Air-safety regulations require airplanes to fly about 1,000 feet higher than helicopters.) Most people prefer helicopter flights because they provide a slower ride and a closer view, but airplane flights allow you to cover more ground in less time—and generally for less money. Note: most carriers offer discounts for children.

Strict regulations govern which parts of the park scenic flights may fly over to reduce noise pollution for other park visitors. Over 75 percent of the park is off limits to scenic flights, including the area above the popular viewpoints on the North and South Rims and the "corridor zone" between them. Furthermore, no aircraft may fly below the rim within the boundaries of the park. Despite these restrictions, scenic flights reveal some of the most remote and beautiful parts of the canyon, many of which are seldom seen by hikers or river runners.

HELICOPTER FLIGHTS ($125–$220)

Airstar Helicopters (866-689-8687, www.airstar.com)
Grand Canyon Helicopters (800-541-4537, www.grandcanyonhelicoptersaz.com)
Papillon (800-528-2418, www.papillon.com)

AIRPLANE FLIGHTS ($90–$200)

Air Grand Canyon (800-247-4726, www.airgrandcanyon.com)
Grand Canyon Airlines (866-235-9422, www.grandcanyonairlines.com)

National Canyon

GEOLOGY

GRAND CANYON is a geological wonderland. There are few locations on the planet with so many eye-popping rock formations on display in a single place. It's safe to say that, had they been located elsewhere, many of these individual rock formations would be world-famous landmarks on their own. But within the depths of the canyon they occur by the dozen. Rainbow-splashed mesas, temples and buttes cascade down from the rim, extending for miles in either direction. Visually, there is so much to see—so many colors, textures, and shadows—that your sense of perspective often melts away. The scope of the scenery is dizzying, which is what makes staring out into Grand Canyon so much fun.

Even if you know nothing about geology, Grand Canyon is still an impressive sight. But take the time to learn about the forces that created it, and you'll look upon the canyon with a fresh set of eyes. Suddenly, what was once amazing will become astounding. What once took your breath away will make your head spin.

On a human timescale Grand Canyon seems ancient, peaceful and serene. On a geologic timescale, however, it is young, violent and exciting. Many people are shocked to discover that Grand Canyon was created in less than 6 million years. When you consider that the earth is over 4.5 *billion* years old, 6 million years seems like the blink of an eye. It's as if northern Arizona suddenly just cracked open and—bam!—there was Grand Canyon.

In reality, northern Arizona was sliced open by the Colorado River. After tumbling down from the Rockies, the Colorado twists and turns through the desert Southwest, picking up an enormous amount of sediment along the way. This sediment—a mixture of gravel, silt and clay eroded from the region's soft rocks—scrapes along the bottom of the river like sandpaper, cutting downward at a rate of about 6.5 inches every 1,000 years. Over the past 5 million years, the Colorado has sliced through northern Arizona like a knife through a wedding cake. In the process it has exposed dozens of layers of progressively older rocks. This gives Grand Canyon one of its most defining characteristics: it is one of the few places in the world where you can view almost 2 billion years of Earth history just by glancing up and down.

The creation of Grand Canyon was a two-step process: the initial laying down of the rocks (which took hundreds of millions of years) and the slicing, downward erosion of the Colorado River (which took less than 6 million years). To fully understand the depth and complexity of the geology of the Grand Canyon, it helps to examine the rock-building process first.

GRAND CANYON ROCKS

MOST ROCKS IN Grand Canyon are sedimentary rocks, which form when sediments such as sand, silt or mud gather in thick layers that, over time, are compressed into rock. Grand Canyon's sedimentary rock layers accumulated over millions of years on the prehistoric surface of northern Arizona, which has been home to giant sand dunes, muddy river deltas, and shallow tropical seas over the past 500 million years. These environments formed as ancient continents drifted across the globe and ancient oceans advanced and retreated over those continents. Eventually, eroded sediments from each of these environments formed distinct layers of sedimentary rocks; sand dunes were cemented into sandstone, mud was compressed into shale, and the discarded shells of marine animals were cemented together into limestone.

Because Grand Canyon's rocks were laid down chronologically, one on top of the other, they reflect a geological relationship known as superposition, which simply states that the rocks above are younger than the rocks below. Move your eyes from the rim to the river and you are essentially staring back into time. At the bottom of the canyon we find the region's oldest exposed rocks: Vishnu Schist and Zoroaster Granite. These two rocks, referred to as the Precambrian Rocks of the Inner Gorge, are the only common rocks in Grand Canyon that are not sedimentary.

Vishnu Schist is a metamorphic rock that formed roughly 1.7 billion years ago when intense heat and pressure transformed previously formed shale into schist. About 200 million years later, magma shot up into cracks in the schist and cooled into Zoroaster Granite, forming beautiful veins of pink granite.

A little over 1 billion years ago, a collection of sedimentary rocks known as the Grand Canyon Supergroup started to form. These rocks were later slightly metamorphosed and tilted at a 20-degree angle, but today they are only visible in a handful of places within the canyon.

It wasn't until about 543 million years ago that the Tapeats Sandstone, the oldest major sedimentary rock in Grand Canyon, started to form. What happened in the 1 billion years between the formation of the Vishnu Schist and the Tapeats Sandstone is a bit of a mystery. During that time, up to 12,000 feet of additional rocks formed on top of the Vishnu Schist. But by 570 million years ago these additional rocks had eroded away, leaving an enormous gap in the geologic record. Geologists refer to such a gap as an unconformity. In Grand Canyon, the gap between the Vishnu Schist and the Tapeats Sandstone is known as the Great Unconformity, a name given by the early explorer John Wesley Powell.

"...the thought grew in my mind that the canyons of this region would be a Book of Revelations in the rock-leaved Bible of geology. The thought fructified and I determined to read the book."

– John Wesley Powell

Great Unconformity

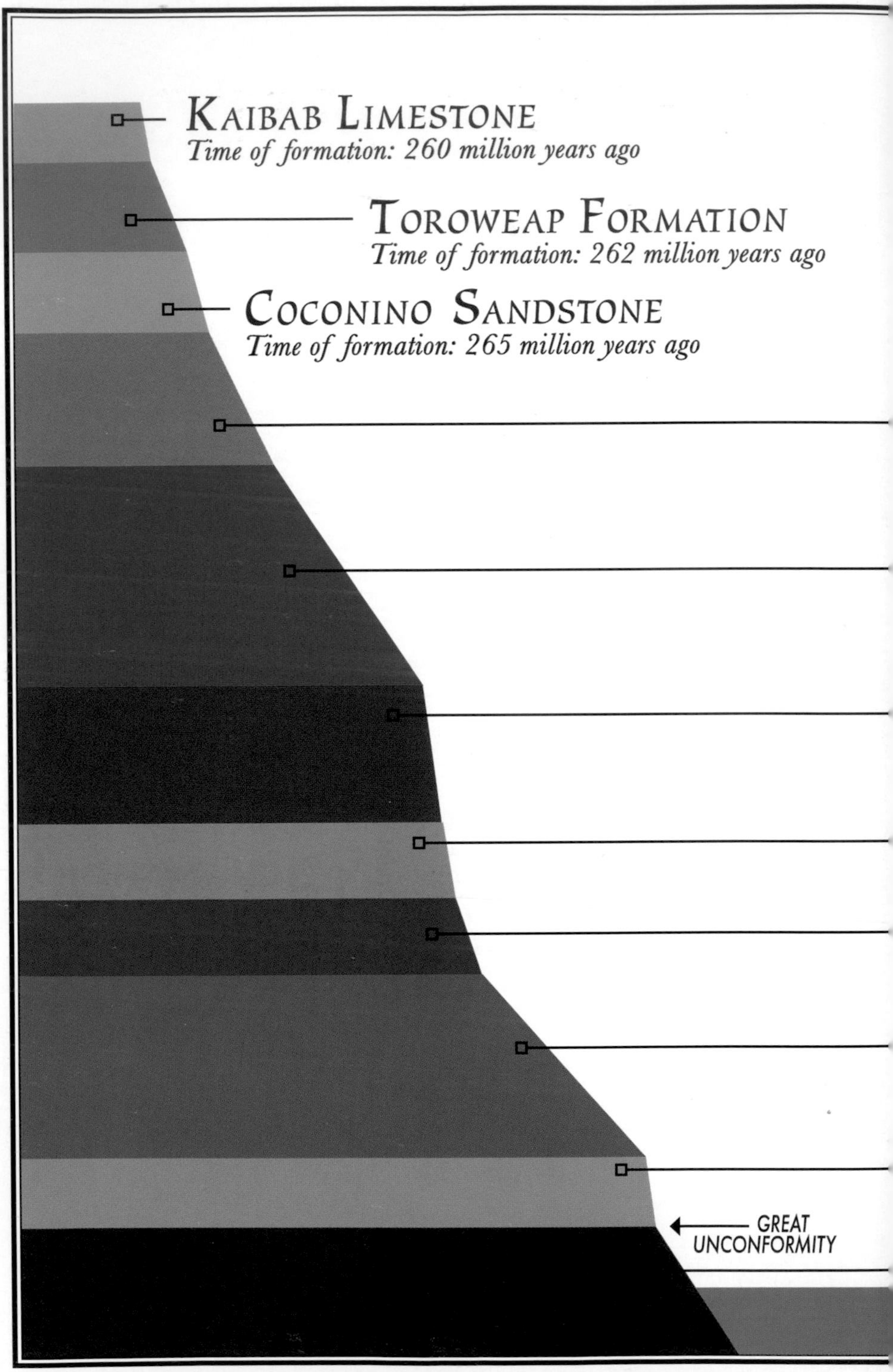
KAIBAB LIMESTONE
Time of formation: 260 million years ago
TOROWEAP FORMATION
Time of formation: 262 million years ago
COCONINO SANDSTONE
Time of formation: 265 million years ago
GREAT UNCONFORMITY

GRAND CANYON
ROCK LAYERS

Hermit Shale
Time of formation: 270 million years ago

Supai Group
Time of formation: 270-320 million years ago

Redwall Limestone
Time of formation: 340 million years ago

Temple Butte Limestone
Time of formation: 370 million years ago

Muav Limestone
Time of formation: 530 million years ago

Bright Angel Shale
Time of formation: 540 million years ago

Tapeats Sandstone
Time of formation: 550 million years ago

Vishnu Schist
Time of formation: 1.7–1.5 billion years ago

THE COLORADO PLATEAU

THE SEDIMENTS THAT ultimately formed the sedimentary rocks in Grand Canyon generally accumulated at or near sea level. So how did they end up thousands of feet *above* sea level? The answer has to do with Grand Canyon's location on the southwestern edge of a huge area known as the Colorado Plateau. This area, filled with some of the most stunning landscapes in America, encompasses much of the Four Corners region, which includes Arizona, Utah, Colorado and New Mexico.

Starting about 60 million years ago, forces within the earth began pushing the Colorado Plateau upward. By about 5 million years ago, the Colorado Plateau had risen over a vertical mile. This higher elevation led to increased precipitation, which led to increased erosion that stripped away many of the region's rocks. Although the Kaibab Limestone—the top-most rock layer in Grand Canyon—was once covered by as much as 10,000 feet of younger rocks, those rocks have long since eroded away. As erosion continued to sculpt the region, it created one of the most stunning landscapes in the world.

Aside from their physical beauty, the sedimentary rocks of Grand Canyon are notable because they are so exquisitely preserved. This is due to the relative stability, geologically speaking, of the Colorado Plateau. As continents have drifted across the globe over the past 600 million years, smashing into one another and deforming the crust of the earth, the Colorado Plateau has remained sheltered from much of the action. As a result, its sedimentary layers have survived relatively intact. By contrast, the rock layers in the geologically active regions surrounding the Colorado Plateau—such as the Great Basin and Rocky Mountains—have been severely deformed.

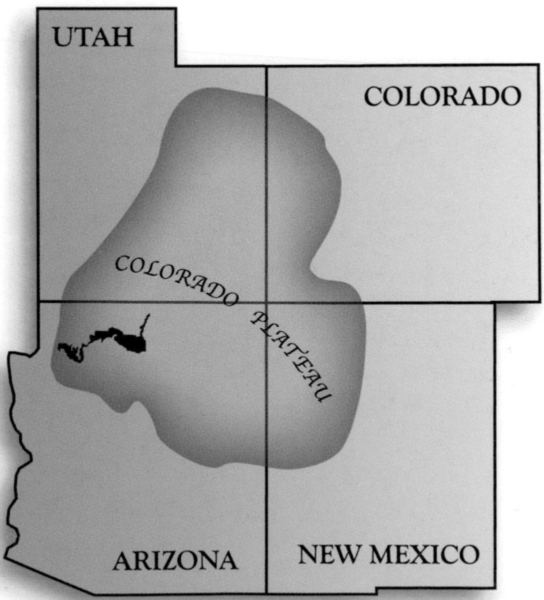

Some geologists believe the Colorado Plateau has resisted deformation so successfully because its crust is so much thicker than the surrounding regions. In places, the crust beneath the Colorado Plateau is up to 25 miles thick. The crust of the Great Basin, by comparison, is only 16 miles thick. So rather

View above the South Rim

than buckle and break as it was pushed upward, the Colorado Plateau has remained relatively unaltered as a single tectonic block.

The uplift of the Colorado Plateau continues today. By some estimates, it has risen as much as 1,000 feet in the past million years. And while much of the region has remained intact, there have been some notable geologic hiccups along its boundaries. In western Grand Canyon, which lies near the boundary of the Colorado Plateau and the Great Basin, the crust is thinner and more broken. As a result, hundreds of volcanoes have erupted near western Grand Canyon over the past 2 million years. At least 150 eruptions have resulted in lava pouring over the rim of the Canyon and tumbling down to the Colorado River. When the lava cooled at the bottom of the Canyon, it often formed massive dams that backed up the river for miles. The largest dam, which geologists have named Prospect Dam, was over 2,300 feet high. It created a massive reservoir that took 22 years to fill and stretched all the way back to Moab, Utah. But in as little as 20,000 years, the Colorado had eroded Prospect Dam—a feat that speaks volumes of the corrosive power of the river.

THE COLORADO RIVER

MORE THAN ANYTHING, erosion by the Colorado River is responsible for the creation of Grand Canyon. But that's only part of the story. The specifics are considerably more complex. Early geologists, starting with John Wesley Powell, made the mistake of assuming that the modern river has always flowed along its present path, and that it was entirely responsible for the creation of Grand Canyon. The way they saw it, the river simply cut down into northern Arizona as the Colorado Plateau rose up around it.

But in the 1930s and '40s, geologists came to the startling conclusion that the Colorado has not always followed its present course. Although the ancestral Colorado did flow into northern Arizona, passing through the region that would one day become eastern Grand Canyon, it avoided western Grand Canyon entirely. Rather than flow west through Arizona, it flowed *north* into Utah. This led to a frustrating dilemma: if the early Colorado avoided western Grand Canyon, how did it form?

This question has yet to be answered definitively. Much of the evidence has long since eroded away, so facts are hard to come by. But geologists have been able to piece together a general theory to explain what happened. It begins with the creation of a "lower" Colorado River that originated somewhere to the west of Grand Canyon. Over time the headwaters of the lower Colorado eroded east until they reached the western edge of the Colorado Plateau. As they continued to carve away at the landscape, they came closer and closer to the upper Colorado. Then, around 5 million years ago, a critical divide was breached between the two rivers. The lower Colorado captured the upper Colorado, and the upper Colorado started flowing west. At that moment, the modern river was born.

For the next 5 million years, the modern Colorado bore down into the landscape as the Colorado Plateau rose up around it—pretty much the way early

> In the 1930s and '40s, geologists came to the startling conclusion that the Colorado has not always followed its present course. Rather than flow west into Arizona, the ancestral Colorado flowed *north* into Utah.

geologists envisioned it. But the river's rate of downward cutting has not been constant. In fact, the cutting has varied considerably depending on which rocks the river cut through. Soft sedimentary rocks, such as shale, were cut through quickly, while harder sedimentary rocks, such as limestone, took much longer.

At any rate, the Colorado cut through all of the sedimentary rocks in a remarkably short period of time. By about 3.8 million years ago, Grand Canyon was within 500 feet of its current depth. The river was now grinding through Vishnu Schist—the hardest rock in the canyon—and its rate of downward cutting slowed significantly. At the same time, another characteristic of the river started to change. As the Colorado ground down the steep obstacles that choked up the river, its grade began to level out. Because rivers with gentle grades are much less erosive than rivers with steep grades, the Colorado's rate of downward cutting was further reduced. Over the past 1 million years, the river has cut down less than 50 feet.

This shocking fact reveals an incredible amount about the creation of Grand Canyon. While the Colorado sliced into northern Arizona like a band saw between 3 and 5 million years ago, it has done relatively little since then. Contrary to popular belief, erosion in Grand Canyon does not occur at a steady rate. Rather, it happens in brief spurts when powerful forces pound away at the landscape. These spurts have almost always corresponded to periods when massive obstacles—lava dams, the uplift of the Colorado Plateau—blocked an easy path for the river. Ultimately, the Colorado not only finds the path of least resistance, it creates it. This gives one pause when considering the ultimate fate of the man-made obstacles (dams) that hold back the river today.

THE CANYON EXPANDS

ALTHOUGH THE COLORADO River is incredibly good at cutting down, it barely makes a dent horizontally. In fact, the river often *adds* inches to the riverbank by depositing sediment. Yet in places the Grand Canyon is over 10 miles wide. What's going on here?

Although the Colorado has carved out a remarkably deep channel, the width of Grand Canyon is the result of runoff from the rim. In both cases the mechanics are similar—gritty water grinding away at the soft rocks, breaking them down into sediment that's ultimately flushed out of the canyon. But while most of the water in the Colorado River arrives from the Rocky Mountains to the east, runoff from the rim falls on northern Arizona in the form of rain and snow. In effect, the Colorado's deep channel serves as a giant template, funneling much of the region's runoff into the Canyon.

But the rate of erosion along Grand Canyon's walls has not been constant. The walls of the North Rim have eroded up to 10 times faster than the walls of the South Rim. This has nothing to do with the rocks that are being eroded—the two rims share the same rocks—but rather the amount of precipitation that tumbles down from each rim. Both sides of the Grand Canyon are tilted slightly to the south. As a result, precipitation that falls on the North Rim runs *into* the canyon, while precipitation that falls on the South Rim runs *away* from the canyon. Because the walls of the North Rim receive so much more runoff, they have eroded at a significantly faster rate. This fact is readily apparent to anyone who has visited both sides of the canyon. Viewed from the South Rim, the North Rim gradually

> Runoff from the North Rim flows into the Canyon, while runoff from the South Rim flows *away* from the Canyon. As a result, the walls of the North Rim have eroded at a significantly faster rate.

recedes into the distance. But viewed from the North Rim, the walls of the South Rim appear as a sheer cliff.

While the rims have eroded at different rates, they both trace a jagged path to the river. Rather than descend steadily, Grand Canyon's walls cascade down in a series of craggy temples and buttes. Again, this is due to varying rates of erosion. Just as the Colorado has cut down through the canyon's rocks at different rates, the same rocks have eroded horizontally at different rates as well. Soft rocks erode easily to form gentle slopes. Hard rocks resist erosion to form steep cliffs. This stair step formation of rock layers is one of the defining characteristics of the Grand Canyon. To frequent hikers, the varying slopes provide a constant reminder of where one is in the Canyon.

Another notable feature of Grand Canyon is its massive side canyons. These often form along faults where the land has lifted or subsided, creating a narrow channel where runoff accumulates. Over time, this runoff carves out a deep side canyon. The process is self-reinforcing; as the side canyon grows bigger, it collects more runoff, leading to bigger side canyons, more runoff, and so on.

Although flowing water causes most erosion in Grand Canyon, other forces are also at work. "Frost wedging" occurs when water freezes and expands in the cracks of rocks, producing incredible pressures—up to 20,000 pounds *per square inch*—that can split rocks apart. In some cases, frost wedging triggers rockfalls that send massive chunks of the Canyon tumbling down towards the river.

Rockfalls also occur when soft rocks erode beneath hard rocks, creating a pronounced overhang that ultimately collapses under its own weight. This process is referred to as slab failure. In Grand Canyon, with its many alternating layers of hard and soft rocks, slab failure is quite common. It's also the reason why the Canyon's hard rock layers erode to form steep cliffs.

Ultimately, the creation of Grand Canyon was due to many factors: billions of years of rock building, erosion, tectonic forces—all conspired to create the stunning landscape now on display. Millions of years from now, those same forces will have altered Grand Canyon beyond recognition. So consider yourself lucky. You're alive at a time when you can explore and learn about one of the great geological wonders of the world.

Tapeats Sandstone in Blacktail Canyon

ECOLOGY

MORE SUBTLE THAN Grand Canyon's geology, but equally fantastic, is the park's ecology. First-time visitors often assume the canyon is barren and lifeless, but this is anything but the case. Over 8,000 feet of sudden elevation change has created a stunning range of life zones all lying remarkably close to one another. Nowhere is this more apparent than on the North Kaibab Trail, which starts in the cool boreal forest of the North Rim and ends up in the scorching desert at the bottom of the canyon. In a matter of hours, hikers pass by spruce trees and cacti, the equivalent of traveling from Canada to Mexico in a single day.

The wide range of biodiversity in Grand Canyon is due, more than anything else, to temperature and precipitation, which are both affected by elevation. Generally speaking, temperatures rise and aridity increases as you descend into the canyon. From the rim to the river, the contrast between environments can be extreme. At the sweltering bottom of western Grand Canyon, an average of six inches of rain falls a year, and only rugged desert plants such as cacti and yucca can survive. The cool, high plateaus of the North Rim, however, often receive over 30 inches of precipitation a year, and they are covered with lush alpine forests.

Not surprisingly, the Canyon's striking range of climates has also affected the distribution of animals. Cold-blooded reptiles that thrive in the warm inner Canyon are much less common on the rim, and rim dwellers that require a steady source of water fare poorly in much of the inner canyon. But the distribution of plants also influences the distribution of animals. Because plants form the foundation of healthy food chains and provide valuable habitat, they play a vital role in determining where certain animals can live.

But in any ecosystem all life forms exist in a continuous cycle of interdependence, each organism affecting the lives of all others. Plants, therefore, are often equally dependent on animals. Consider the relationship between the pinyon pine and a bird called the pinyon jay. Pinyon pines produce large seeds that, unlike some plant seeds, are too heavy to be dispersed by the wind. But the seeds are a staple of the pinyon jay's diet. After gathering the nuts, the bird buries them for later use, and some uneaten seeds ultimately grow into new trees. Thus, pinyon pines provide the jays with an important source of food, and the pinyon jays ensure a healthy population of pines.

When viewed as a whole, the plants and animals of a particular area form unique, interdependent communities that ecologists call "biotic communities." From tropical rain forests to frozen Arctic tundra, biotic communities are found in every corner of the world. In Grand Canyon we find six major biotic communities: boreal forests, ponderosa forests, pinyon-juniper woodland, desert scrub, and the lush riparian habitat along the banks of the Colorado River. With the exception of the riparian habitat, which follows the course of the Colorado, these biotic communities generally form horizontal bands across Grand Canyon.

Because elevation has such a profound affect on climate, it seems reasonable to assume that biotic communities could be mapped out simply on elevation. But this is not the case. Although elevation provides a rough approximation of where certain biotic communities will occur, many local environmental factors come into play. And many plants and animals can live in more than one biotic community. In Grand Canyon, where a large number of biotic communities are packed into a relatively small space, the boundaries between them are often blurred.

Biotic communities are also affected by microclimates, small pockets of temperature and moisture that vary dramatically from their immediate surroundings. Microclimates are caused by a variety of environmental factors including local topography, proximity to water, and exposure to sunlight. For example, south-facing slopes receive much more sunlight than north-facing slopes, making them significantly warmer and drier, even at higher elevations. This explains why desert plants such as yucca are found at high elevations on the south-facing North Rim, while shady pockets along the South Rim support small populations of Douglas-fir, a tree that generally avoids the South Rim's warmer, drier climate.

C. HART MERRIAM

The concept of biotic communities, i.e. "life zones" where specific groups of plants and animals interact, was first developed at Grand Canyon by the biologist C. Hart Merriam. In 1889 Merriam, then director of the U.S. Biological Survey, led an expedition to Grand Canyon to study the region's plants and animals. As he descended into the canyon, he noticed distinct communities of plants and animals living together. He called these communities "life zones," and theorized that their location was due to the different temperature zones they occupied. Although additional research would show that life zones are dependant on much more than temperature alone, Merriam's Grand Canyon expedition was the first time a scientist had studied plants and animals living *together* in a quantifiable way. His groundbreaking work paved the way for the study of modern ecology.

Grand Canyon Weather

Located in the arid Southwest, Grand Canyon receives much less precipitation than most parts of the country. Although minimal, the Canyon's precipitation arrives in a fairly predictable pattern, falling in the winter and the summer in a nearly 50/50 split.

In the summer, prevailing winds arrive from the south, bringing moisture from the Gulf of California. As the moist air passes over Arizona, it's lifted up and over the highlands just south of Grand Canyon, arriving at the Canyon cool and condensed. In the morning, when the sun heats the inner canyon, hot air rises up and collides with the cool, moist air above. This sudden collision creates short-lived afternoon thunderstorms. In July, August and early September (monsoon season), these storms pound Grand Canyon on an almost daily basis.

In the winter, prevailing winds arrive from the west or northwest, bringing moist air from the Pacific. But the vast majority of this moisture is wrung out by the Sierra Nevada Mountains. What little moisture remains eventually finds its way into northern Arizona. Although winter storms in Grand Canyon are much less intense than summer storms, they can often linger for days.

In the spring and the fall Grand Canyon becomes extremely arid, resulting in dramatic temperature swings. During the day, the dry air allows up to 90 percent of solar radiation to reach the ground. (Humid areas, by contrast, only receive about 40 percent.) At night, the situation is reversed; 90 percent of the canyon's accumulated heat is radiated back into the atmosphere through clear, dry skies. (In humid areas, heat is often reflected back by an insulating cloud cover.)

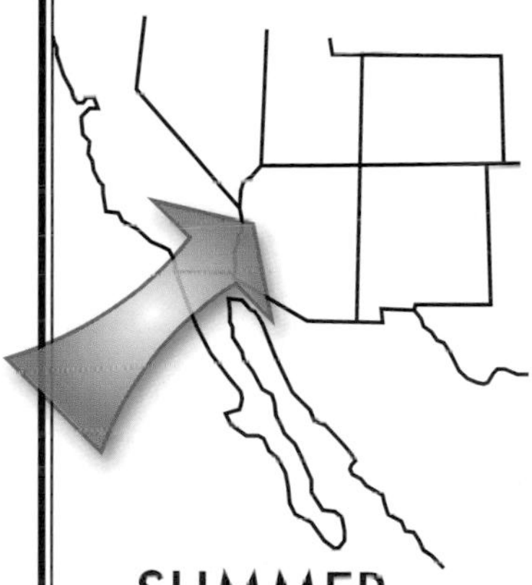

SUMMER

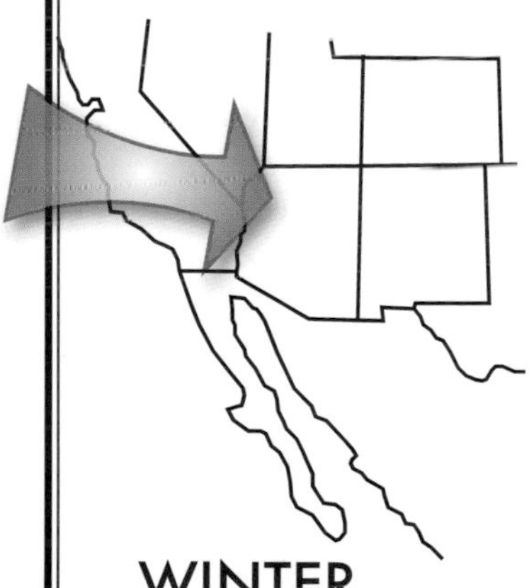

WINTER

ICE AGE in Grand Canyon

Twenty thousand years ago, near the peak of the last Ice Age, Grand Canyon was a much different place. Although the topography was nearly identical, the distribution of plants and animals would have been unrecognizable to modern eyes. During the last Ice Age, a cool, wet climate descended over the Southwest that forced many plants and animals to retreat to lower, warmer elevations. Juniper trees, which currently grow on the South Rim, grew along the banks of the Colorado River, and Douglas-fir, a tree currently found only in the park's highest elevations, grew on the Tonto Platform—3,000 feet below the rim.

Many strange and wonderful creatures also roamed the region during this time, including camels, horses and Merriam's teratorn, a bird with a wingspan more t[illegible]feet across. Perhaps the most notable creature was the Shasta ground sloth, a massive lumbering animal that stood seven feet tall and weighed up to 400 pounds. Sadly, around 10,000 years ago many of these large prehistoric animals went extinct, most likely due to overhunting by early human settlers.

As the glaciers that covered much of North America retreated between 15,000 and 10,000 years ago, the Ice Age drew to a close. In the Southwest temperatures rose, and plants and animals living in the Inner Canyon began a slow migration towards the rim. The remarkable flexibility of Grand Canyon's plants and animals—retreating to the Canyon's depths when temperatures drop, climbing back up when they warm—is a powerful reminder that the park's seemingly fixed life zones are, in fact, highly dynamic and adaptable.

Air currents also affect microclimates. During the day, as the sun beats down on the region, hot air rises up the canyon walls. Then, at night, cool air flows down from the rim. These invisible rivers of air allow a wide range of plants to survive in unlikely places along the Canyon's walls.

Although life zone boundaries are often blurred by Grand Canyon's unique topography, the Canyon can also act as a formidable barrier to plant and animal movement. Consider the Abert squirrel, a small, grayish squirrel that lives exclusively in ponderosa pine forests and is entirely dependent on ponderosas as a source of food. During the last Ice Age, when the climate was much cooler and wetter, ponderosa forests stretched across much of northern Arizona, including the inner Grand Canyon. For thousands of years Abert squirrels roamed throughout these forests, but when temperatures started to rise around 10,000 years ago the ponderosa pines retreated to higher elevations. Trees growing in the depths of the Canyon moved up to the rims, and with them came the Abert squirrels. Some squirrels retreated to the South Rim, and some retreated to the North Rim, creating two isolated populations on either side of the canyon. Over time, the squirrels living on the North Rim developed unique physical characteristics—most notably a striking white tail—that have led scientists to classify them as an entirely separate subspecies called the Kaibab squirrel.

More recently, humans have impacted Grand Canyon's ecology. When miners abandoned their search for Grand Canyon riches in the late 1800s, they often left burros behind. These pack animals, originally from the deserts of Africa, were rugged enough to survive on their own, and soon they were breeding and multiplying. A century later, there were as many as 350 feral burros living in Grand Canyon. Conservation groups became concerned that the burros were competing with the Canyon's already-threatened population of bighorn sheep for scarce resources, and in the late 1970s the burros were rounded up one by one and transported out of the Canyon. But many feral burro populations remain throughout the Southwest. In recent years, there have been scattered reports of new feral burro populations in western Grand Canyon.

The interaction between plants, animals and landscapes is incredibly complex in any environment. But in Grand Canyon, one of the most dynamic environments in the world, this complexity is brought to new heights. At times, it can be overwhelming. Even seasoned naturalists sometimes find themselves struggling to comprehend the sophisticated ecology of the park. But Grand Canyon also presents a tremendous opportunity for study and exploration. You could easily spend a lifetime learning about the ecology of the park, which is what keeps many nature lovers coming back year after year.

BALD EAGLE

Haliaeetus leucocephalus

Bald Eagles range over much of North America, including Alaska and Mexico. At one time there may have been as many as 75,000 bald eagles in the lower 48 states, but by the early 1960s there were fewer than 900. Hunting and habitat loss had eliminated bald eagles throughout much of their natural range. In 1967 bald eagles were placed on the federal Endangered Species List, and since then they have made a remarkable comeback. There are now roughly 30,000 bald eagles in the lower 48 states and an additional 40,000 in Alaska. Although bald eagles range over a vast territory, most return to nest within 100 miles of where they were raised. Nests are reused year after year and are added to annually (some can reach up to 10 feet across and weigh up to 2,000 pounds). Bald eagles do not develop their distinctive white head until their fourth or fifth year. The "bald" in "bald eagle" is derived from an old English word meaning white. The bald eagle's scientific name, *Haliaeetus leucocephalus*, means "white-headed sea eagle."

U.S. RANGE

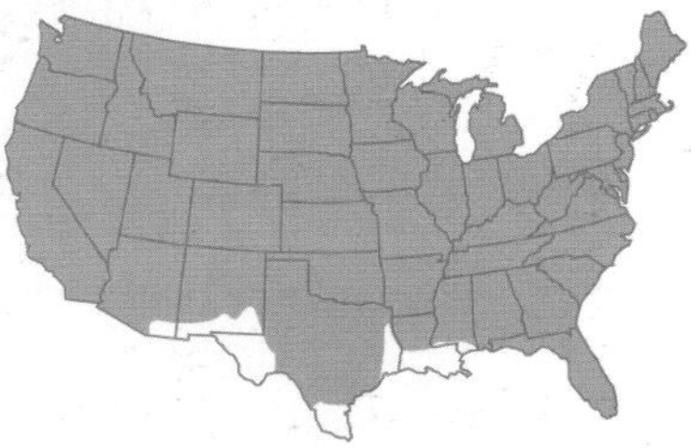

Found throughout Grand Canyon

INFO

Wingspan: 8 feet

Length: 40 inches

Weight: 14 pounds

Lifespan: 30 years

Population: 70,000

BIGHORN SHEEP

Ovis canadensis

Bighorn sheep inhabit the steep cliffs of Grand Canyon where they use their sure-footed climbing skills to avoid predators. Although they can weigh up to 300 pounds, they are capable of jumping down 20-foot inclines with grace. Both sexes grow horns, but the ram's are particularly impressive, twisting up and around the ears in a C-shaped curl. A large pair can weigh up to 30 pounds and reach 33 inches in length. Horns grow longer each year, but if they ever start to block peripheral vision they are *broomed*—deliberately rubbed down on rocks. During mating season in the fall, rams establish dominance through repeated butting contests in which they charge each other head-on at speeds topping 20 miles per hour. When their horns smash together it produces a loud crack that can often be heard for miles. Thickened skulls let them withstand repeated collisions, and males with the biggest horns generally do the most mating. Over the past century, hunting and diseases from domestic sheep have taken a significant toll on bighorn populations in Grand Canyon.

U.S. RANGE

Found on rocky cliffs in Grand Canyon

INFO

Weight: 250 pounds

Shoulder Height: 3–4 feet

Length: 5–6 feet

Tracks: 

BOBCAT

Lynx rufus

Bobcats are North America's most common wildcat, but they are elusive animals that are rarely seen or heard. They generally lay low during the day, then wander for miles at night. The bobcat is closely related to the lynx, which is larger and found in colder environments. The name *bobcat* comes from the cat's stubby "bobbed" tail. Bobcats are only slightly larger than house cats, and they share many of the same personality traits: hissing, purring, and sometimes using trees as scratching posts. Bobcats prey on a wide range of animals including deer, rabbits, squirrels, small birds, and snakes, but they rarely chase their prey. Instead, bobcats seek out a hiding spot and lie patiently in wait, pouncing when a victim approaches. Bobcats are extremely solitary animals; males and females come together only for mating. Females usually have litters of two or three kittens, although they can have as many as seven. Recent evidence indicates that bobcat populations are stable and may be increasing in places.

U.S. RANGE

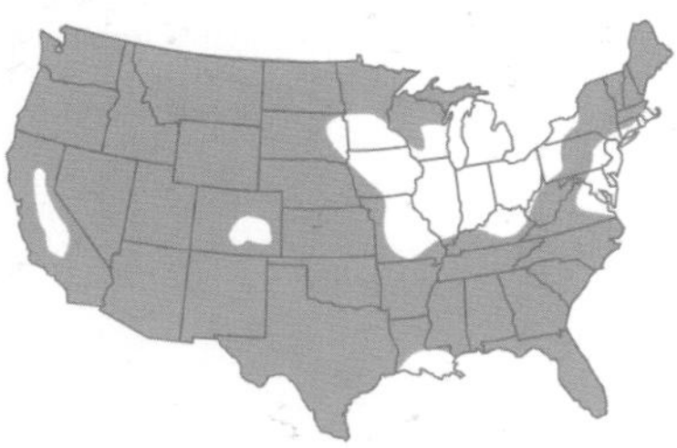

Found throughout Grand Canyon

INFO

Weight: 15–30 pounds

Shoulder Height: 1.5–2 feet

Length: 3–4 feet

Tracks: 

CALIFORNIA CONDOR

Gymnogyps californianus

California condors are the largest and most spectacular birds in Grand Canyon. Although their historic range once extended from British Columbia to Mexico, by 1982 the worldwide California condor population had plummeted to 22 birds. Habitat loss, shootings, and birds feeding on poisonous lead-shot in carcasses left by hunters decimated condor populations. With the species at the brink of extinction, the last remaining birds were captured and bred in captivity. Then, in the 1990s, condors were reintroduced to central California and Grand Canyon. Although captive-bred condors have done remarkably well in the Grand Canyon, it remains to be seen if they can successfully reproduce in the wild. Condor reproduction is a slow process—condors do not reach sexual maturity until six years of age, and an adult pair typically raises only one chick every other year. But there are encouraging signs. In 2003 a condor chick that hatched in the park fledged—the first known occurrence in Arizona in over 100 years. Adult condors can be spotted soaring in the thermals above Grand Canyon. Although they are easily confused with turkey vultures, condors have much larger wingspans and triangular white coloring on the underside of their wings.

U.S. RANGE

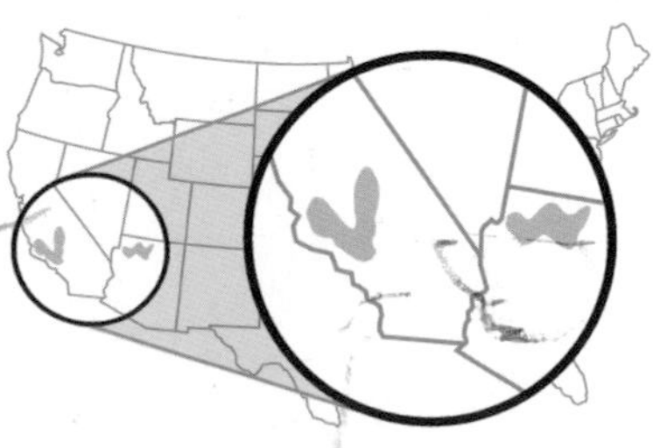

Found throughout Grand Canyon

INFO

Wingspan: 10 feet

Weight: 20 pounds

Lifespan: 60 years

Southwest Population: ~40

Total Population: ~200

ELK

Cervus elaphus

Elk are the largest member of the deer family found on the Colorado Plateau. They are distinguished from mule deer by their massive size and dark brown coloration above the neck. Although elk often appear docile, they can be dangerous during rutting season and should never be approached. Shawnee Indians call elk *wapiti*, "White Rump," but a male elk's most distinguishing characteristic is its massive antlers. Antlers are only found on bulls. They are shed each year in the spring, and over the next three to four months new antlers grow back at the rate of about a half inch a day. Antlers can grow several feet across and weigh up to 50 pounds, reaching maximum size in time for the fall rut. During rutting season, bulls emit a bugle-like sound as a sign of dominance and a challenge to other bulls. The bugle starts off as a bellow and changes to a shrill scream that can often be heard for miles. Dominance between bulls is determined in rutting contests where elk clash antlers with one another. The most dominant bulls have been known to assemble harems of up to 60 females.

U.S. RANGE

Found on the North and South Rim

INFO

Weight: 600–1,000 pounds

Shoulder Height: 4.5–5 feet

Length: 6–9 feet

Tracks:

MOUNTAIN LION

Felis concolor

Mountain lions, also known as pumas or cougars, have the most extensive range of any North American mammal—stretching from Canada to Argentina. At one time they inhabited all 48 lower states, but in the late 1800s and early 1900s mountain lions in the United States were hunted to the brink of extinction. Following strict hunting regulations, they have made a steady comeback in some wilderness areas, especially the Four Corners region. Mountain lions are the largest wildcats in North America. They are quick, efficient killers that can travel up to 25 miles a day in search of prey. A mountain lion will generally stalk animals to within 30 feet before attacking. When they pounce they can leap up to 20 feet in a single bound, killing their victims by inflicting a lethal bite that severs the spinal cord. Mountain lions feed primarily on deer, killing up to one a week. They also feed on elk, coyotes, and bighorn sheep. Mountain lions are almost never seen in the park, but use extreme caution if you encounter one. Although there has never been an attack in Grand Canyon National Park, they have been known to attack humans elsewhere.

U.S. RANGE

Found in remote areas in Grand Canyon

INFO

Weight: 100–200 pounds

Shoulder Height: 4.5–5 feet

Length: 6–9 feet

Tracks: 

MULE DEER

Odocoileus hemionus

Mule deer are the most commonly spotted large mammal in the park. They are frequently seen grazing near the railroad tracks in Grand Canyon Village. Although closely related to white-tailed deer, mule deer are slightly larger and have white tails with a black tip. Mule deer are found predominantly in mountainous areas of the arid Southwest. They are named for their large ears that move independently of each other, like mule ears. Bucks grow antlers that are shed each winter. Although conflict between bucks is infrequent, mild fights sometimes break out. During these fights antlers are enmeshed while each buck tries to force the head of the other down. Injuries are rare, but if the antlers become locked both bucks will be unable to feed and will ultimately die of starvation. Fights between does are much more common. As a result, family groups tend to be spaced widely apart. Young does give birth to one fawn, but older does often give birth to twins. Fawns are able to distinguish their mother from other does through a unique odor produced by glands on the mother's hind legs.

U.S. RANGE

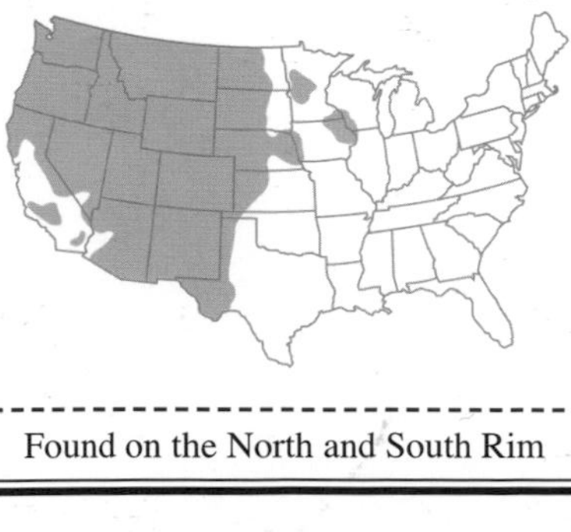

Found on the North and South Rim

INFO

Weight: 150–200 pounds

Shoulder Height: 3–3.5 feet

Length: 5–7 feet

Tracks: 

PERAGRINE FALCON

Falco peregrinus

Peregrine falcons are birds of prey that can spot victims from thousands of feet above. Once a target is selected, a peregrine will dive bomb it at speeds topping 200 mph. The collision creates an explosion of feathers, and victims that don't die immediately upon impact have their necks broken by the peregrine's specially designed beak. Peregrines are such successful strikers that they were used to kill Nazi carrier pigeons in World War II. By the early 1970s, however, peregrine falcons were at the brink of extinction. Hunting, habitat loss, and the extinction of the passenger pigeon (an important source of food) had reduced the worldwide population to less than 40 pairs. To save the remaining birds, young peregrines were raised in captivity and released in the wild. In 1999 peregrines were removed from the federal Endangered Species List. There are currently over 1,650 breeding pairs in the United States and Canada.

U.S. RANGE

Found on tall cliffs in Grand Canyon

INFO

Wingspan: 41 inches

Length: 16 inches

Weight: 1.6 pounds

Lifespan: 15 years

Population: 3,300

RATTLESNAKES

Crotalus scutulatus (below), Crotalus viridis abyssus (right)

There are six species of rattlesnakes in Grand Canyon, including the Mojave Rattlesnake (above) and Grand Canyon Rattlesnake (right). Rattlesnakes are the only venomous snakes in the canyon, but they are seldom seen above the rim. Although they have poor eyesight, they have a sharp sense of smell and can detect body heat through infrared sensors located on either side of their head. These keen senses are used to detect prey while a rattler lies in wait. When the rattler strikes, it injects a paralyzing venom through sharp fangs. Once the victim is motionless, the rattler swallows it whole. Rattlers, in turn, are preyed upon by coyotes, eagles and hawks. Hawks will pluck rattlers from the ground, then drop them repeatedly from the air until the snake is dead. The inner Grand Canyon is the only place in the world where the Grand Canyon Rattlesnake, a subspecies of the Western Rattlesnake, is found. It evolved over millions of years in the confines of the canyon. The Grand Canyon Rattler is distinguished by its pale, pinkish coloration, and irregular, dark blotches that become paler toward the center.

U.S. RANGE

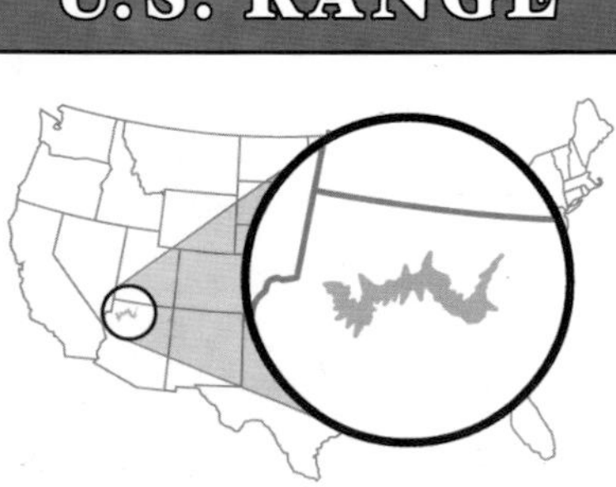

Grand Canyon Rattlesnake

INFO

Mojave Rattlesnake

HUMPBACK CHUB

Gila cypha

The humpback chub is Grand Canyon's most famous native fish. It first appeared 3–5 million years ago in the whitewater-filled canyons of the Colorado River Basin. Because it evolved in swift, muddy waters, the chub has developed some remarkable biological adaptations. Large fins allow it to easily maneuver rapids, small eyes protect it from silt, and when swift water passes over its pronounced hump, the fish is forced down toward the bottom of the river where the current is less strong, helping it stay put during floods. The humpback chub once thrived in the Colorado, but the fish are now on the verge of extinction due to dams, which have significantly lowered water temperatures in the river. Although chubs can survive in cold water, they need warm water to spawn. Today they are forced to spawn in a handful of smaller tributaries. The new Colorado has also allowed non-native species such as trout to invade the chub's natural habitat, competing for resources and feeding on young chub. Although scattered chub populations exist above Lake Powell, the largest remaining chub population—less than 2,000 fish—lives in Grand Canyon near the junction of the Little Colorado River.

U.S. RANGE

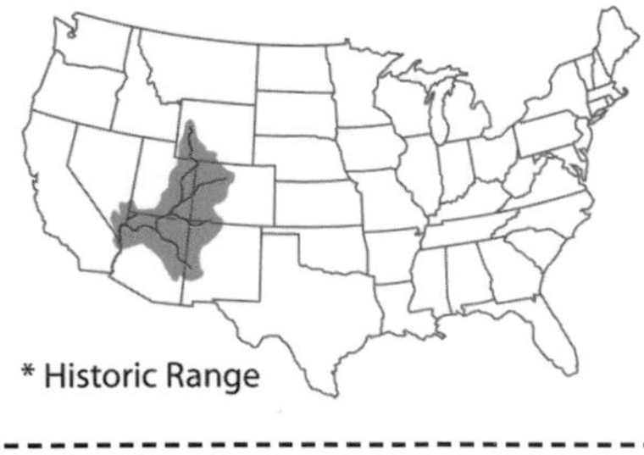

Found only in Colorado River Basin

INFO

Length: 18 inches

Weight: 2 pounds

Color: green/silver/white

Lifespan: 30+ years

RAINBOW TROUT

Oncorhynchus mykiss

Rainbow trout are one of the world's most prized sport fish. They have an olive/bluish back and a characteristic pink band running down their sides. Although they are native to rivers in the western United States, rainbow trout are extremely adaptable. Over the past century they have been transplanted to rivers in Africa, Japan, Southeast Asia, South America, Europe, Australia, and New Zealand. Rainbow trout were introduced to the Colorado River just north of the Grand Canyon following the completion of Glen Canyon Dam in 1964. The cool, clear waters released from the bottom of the dam created an ideal trout habitat. After it was stocked, it became a world-famous fishery, but some of the trout have found their way downstream to the confluence of the Colorado River and the Little Colorado River—a vital spawning ground for native fish. To prevent the trout from feeding on young native fish, federal employees have recently instituted an aggressive trout removal policy. Trout are shocked with electro-fishing gear, captured and euthanized. The carcasses are then given to local Indians for use as fertilizer.

U.S. RANGE

Found in rivers throughout the U.S.

INFO

Length: 10–40 inches

Weight: up to 10 pounds

Color: olive/pink/silver

Lifespan: 6 years

HISTORY

HUMANS FIRST SET eyes on Grand Canyon roughly 10,000 years ago, when primitive hunters and gatherers first arrived in Arizona. Little is known about these prehistoric people, but small artifacts found in the backs of caves confirm their existence in Grand Canyon. Among the objects discovered were spear points and small split-twig figurines twisted into the shapes of animals. Some of the animal figurines were pierced with tiny spears made of agave thorns, indicating that hunting played an important role in their lives.

What ultimately happened to these early settlers is unclear. It's possible that they abandoned Grand Canyon, but it's just as likely that they stayed. In either case, a new culture called the Ancestral Puebloans (Anasazi) appeared several thousand years later. The Ancestral Puebloans occupied the Four Corners region from roughly A.D. 0 to 1200, and for over a thousand years they flourished in Grand Canyon, which marked the westernmost range of their territory.

Ancestral Puebloans have since been subdivided into two distinct cultural groups. The earlier group, the Basketmakers, lived from A.D. 0 to 700. Named for their exceptional skill at basketry, they wove plant fibers into beautiful baskets and sandals. Because they were hunters and gatherers, they were constantly on the move in search of food. But as time passed they discovered agriculture, which allowed them to settle down in one place. Soon they were constructing dwellings in caves or under overhanging cliffs, growing beans, corn and squash nearby.

Although farming was the Basketmakers' main source of food, they also hunted animals with spears, which provided them with both food and the raw materials for clothing. In the winter the Basketmakers wore robes made of deer skin, rabbit skin or turkey feathers. In the summer they wore loin clothes and skirts woven from plant fibers. Jewelry was made from seashells imported along trade routes from the Pacific Coast, and live parrots were imported from Mexico. The Basketmakers kept dogs as pets, smoked tobacco from pipes, and played music on six-hole flutes. By A.D. 600 they had also learned to make pottery, but more striking cultural advances were yet to come.

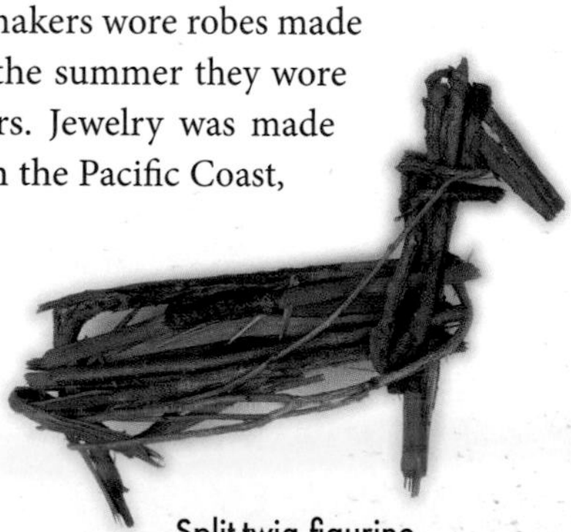

Split-twig figurine

Around A.D 700 the Basketmakers discovered the bow and arrow, which allowed them to hunt more food in less time. With more free time on their hands they continued to advance technologically, and soon they were using stone masonry to build impressive stone villages under the awnings of cliffs. Some of these dwellings, such as Canyon de Chelly in northeast Arizona and Chaco Canyon in New Mexico, are among of the most spectacular archaeological ruins in America.

As Ancestral Puebloan living quarters advanced, so did the rules governing their society. Customs and social codes became highly developed, with some villages operating like independent city-states. These social advances were so profound that archaeologists have subdivided these later Ancestral Puebloans into a second cultural group: the Pueblo Anasazi.

The Pueblo Anasazi built irrigation ditches near fertile areas and stored excess crops in granaries (stone storage compartments). Artistic achievements also blossomed during this time; cotton was spun and woven into beautiful clothes, dwellings were covered with murals and pictographs, and elaborate costumes were used in religious ceremonies.

By A.D. 1100 the Ancestral Puebloans were flourishing, occupying thousands of sites in and around Grand Canyon. Their technological achievements were extraordinary, placing them among the most advanced Indians north of Mexico. Then, at the height of their prosperity, the Ancestral Puebloans mysteriously abandoned their settlements and vanished from Grand Canyon.

Archaeologists are at a loss to explain this sudden departure. Some believe the Ancestral Puebloans fell victim to a massive drought. Others blame a depletion of natural resources. Still others think there was a great war between neighboring tribes. Unfortunately, scant evidence remains to provide a clear picture of what actually happened. Whatever the cause, after abandoning Grand Canyon many Ancestral Puebloans moved south and merged with the Hopi and Zuni tribes. Within a few centuries, other tribes including the Havasupai, Hualapai, Southern Paiute and Navajo had settled the surrounding territory.

Ancestral Puebloan Pottery

Mystery of the Ancestral Puebloans

THE SWIFT DECLINE of the Ancestral Puebloans is one of the Southwest's greatest archaeological mysteries. Why would a culture at the height of its prosperity—by many accounts the most advanced culture north of Mexico—suddenly abandon its settlements? What caused them to flee the Four Corners region they had occupied for over 1,000 years, never to return?

For decades archaeologists believed the Ancestral Puebloans simply fell victim to a massive drought. The entire Southwest experienced a period of decreased rainfall in the late 1200s, and it seemed logical to connect this period to the ancient culture's demise. But recent evidence suggests this so-called Great Drought may not have been enough to cause a complete cultural collapse. The Ancestral Puebloans, it turns out, started to abandon their settlements *prior* to the drought. And they had survived worse droughts in the past. Why should this one be different?

Some archaeologists believe the abandonment was triggered not by a drought, but by a depletion of the region's scarce natural resources, which could have led to social and political upheaval—possibly even war. In fact, many Ancestral Puebloan structures built near the end appear to be defensive in nature.

But if there was a war, why didn't the winners stay to enjoy the spoils? Some archaeologists believe that it wasn't war that brought down the Ancestral Puebloans but a religious collapse. Religion and daily life were one and the same to the Ancestral Puebloans, and a collapse of one would have inevitably led to a collapse of the other. Faced with failing crops, chronic shortages, and rain dances that no longer worked, the Ancestral Puebloans may have lost faith in their prevailing religion. At the same time, the Hopi's new Katsina religion was gaining momentum to the south. With its colored masks and lurid dances, the Katsina movement may have lured the Ancestral Puebloans away from their homeland. Some archaeologists have even speculated that the Ancestral Puebloans may have moved as far away as Mexico.

While these theories offer possible explanations, many unanswered questions remain. Until new evidence comes to light, the Ancestral Puebloans' abandonment will continue to be one of the Canyon's best-kept secrets.

Arizona Tribes

HOPI

The Hopi are one of the oldest tribes in the region, having occupied northeast Arizona for over 1,000 years. Oraibi, a Hopi village 80 miles east of Grand Canyon, was settled over 800 years ago, making it the oldest continuously inhabited town in the United States. Grand Canyon is a deeply symbolic place for the Hopi, who believe that both people and animals emerged from the Grand Canyon at a place called the *Sipaapuni*, a mineral spring located near the junction of the Colorado and Little Colorado Rivers. Hopi religion revolves around *Katsinas*, spirit beings who visit Hopi villages for a few months each year, performing good deeds, punishing criminals, and bringing rain. The Hopi craft hundreds of brightly painted wooden dolls, called *Tihu*, to represent different Katsinas. Tihu (also called Kachina Dolls) are traditionally carved from a single piece of cottonwood root and given to children to teach them about the different Katsinas.

SOUTHERN PAIUTE

The Southern Paiute settled the plateau country north of Grand Canyon around A.D. 1300. Because of the region's limited resources, they found it easier to exist in small bands rather than large groups governed by complex social structures. Each band had an individual leader who acted as a tribal advisor. The leader was generally an elderly man who had spent a lifetime studying the landscape, and he imparted his knowledge of plants and animals to others. The Southern Paiute hunted deer and small game on the Kaibab Plateau, which encompasses much of the North Rim. *Kaibab* is derived from a Paiute word meaning "Mountain Lying Down." While the men hunted, women gathered plants. Over time, the Southern Paiute adopted agriculture from the nearby Hopi and Navajo tribes.

HAVASUPAI

The Havasupai have been living in western Grand Canyon for over 700 years. The name Havasupai, "People of the Blue-Green Water," is a reference to the beautiful turquoise pools and waterfalls found in Havasu Canyon. Because they had access to constant water, the Havasupai grew more food than any other tribe in the region. Havasu Creek, one of the most dependable water sources in Grand Canyon, helped the Havasupai weather even the greatest droughts.

The Hualapai, "Pine Tree People," were close neighbors of the Havasupai. Although listed as two separate tribes by early American explorers, the Havasupai and Hualapai consider themselves members of the same Pai culture. The Hualapai spent most of their time in the forested plateaus above Grand Canyon, but in the summer they would sometimes gather plants in the rugged side canyons along the South Rim.

NAVAJO

The Navajo were one of the last tribes to settle the Grand Canyon region, arriving from northwest Canada sometime between 500 and 1,000 years ago. Upon reaching the desert they were forced to adopt a new way of life. Unable to survive on their own, they resorted to raiding the villages of previously settled tribes. Eventually, however, they learned agriculture from their neighbors. Traditional Navajo homes are called *hogans*, one-room buildings built out of logs and tree branches that always face east so the Navajo can start each day by greeting the light of the rising sun. The Navajo believe that humans must live in harmony with nature, achieving a sense of place called *hozho*. They refer to themselves *Dine*, "The People." In the 1600s the Spanish introduced sheep to the Navajo. Before long, Navajo culture revolved around sheep herding. Sheep meat replaced deer meat as the primary source of protein in the Navajo diet, and sheep wool was woven into beautiful rugs with colorful designs. Navajo legend speaks of two animal beings, Spider Man and Spider Woman, who taught the Navajo how to build looms and weave.

Coronado expedition

A FABLED CITY OF GOLD

LESS THAN 30 years after Columbus discovered North America, Spanish conquistador Hernan Cortez defeated the Aztecs in Mexico. At the time Spain was the most powerful country in the world. Its sprawling empire covered much of Europe and stretched across the Atlantic. But maintaining these far-flung properties was an expensive proposition, and despite the vast wealth plundered from the Aztecs, Spain was soon desperate for additional funds.

Then, in 1529, a Spanish vessel shipwrecked off the Texas coast. The wreck's four survivors spent the next seven years wandering the desert, and when they finally returned to Mexico they told stories of a fabulous city of gold located somewhere in the American Southwest. This city, referred to as the Seven Cities of Cibola, quickly captured the imagination of the Spanish crown.

In 1540 Spanish authorities assembled a military expedition to locate the Seven Cities of Cibola. Led by a charismatic 29-year-old named Francisco Vasquez de Coronado, the expedition consisted of 300 Spanish men, several hundred Indians, and thousands of cattle, sheep and goats. Five months later the expedition reached the spot where the Seven Cities were rumored to be located. All they found was a small Indian village.

Coronado was dejected, but the Indians told him of a larger group of seven cities to the west. Coronado immediately dispatched his lieutenant, Don Pedro de Tovar, to investigate these claims. When Tovar returned he reported that he had failed to locate the Seven Cites of Cibola, but he had learned of mighty river to the west. Hoping this river was the gateway to Cibola, Coronado dispatched another search party under the command of Garcia Lopez de Cardenas.

After three weeks of travel Cardenas' party reached the South Rim. They were the first whites to set eyes on Grand Canyon—and they were hardly impressed. From their vantage point on the South Rim—believed to be somewhere between Moran Point and Desert View—the Spaniards estimated the Colorado River to be just six feet wide. (The average width of the Colorado in Grand Canyon is closer to *300 feet.*) Although their Hopi guides insisted that the river was much larger, the Spaniards refused to believe them. They had never encountered a natural structure of this scale, and they were unable to comprehend its true dimensions.

For three days the Spaniards tried to find a route to the river. One group of soldiers made it a third of the way down, but they were unable to descend any further. Even at that depth, they were shocked to learn that rocks that appeared no more than a few feet high from the rim were actually taller than the 185-foot tower of Seville in Spain. Suddenly comprehending the true size of Grand Canyon, Cardenas turned his men around. Coronado's expedition ultimately traveled as far as present-day Kansas, but the Seven Cities of Cibola were never found.

THE SECOND SPANISH WAVE

IN THE DECADES following Coronado's expedition, Spain once again ignored the Southwest. No colonization attempts were made until 1598, when Jaun de Onate founded Santa Fe, New Mexico. Within a few decades, Spanish missions had spread west towards Hopi towns.

The Hopi deeply resented the proselytizing missionaries. They had no interest in changing their religious beliefs, and they did not want the Spaniards interfering in their daily lives. Before long, Indian mistrust had reached a breaking point. In 1680 leaders from several tribes met in secret to plan a coordinated revolt against the Spanish. The Pueblo Revolt, as it was later called, drove out the Spanish and allowed the Indians to regain control of their territories. But their victory was short-lived. Twelve years later a more powerful Spanish army marched north to reconquer the Southwest. The Hopi retreated to the tops of tall mesas, which were easily defended from above, and before long Hopi mesas had become a favored refuge for Indians fleeing the Spanish throughout the Southwest.

While battles raged to the east of Grand Canyon, Indians living in the remote western Grand Canyon remained relatively undisturbed. Then, in 1776, a Franciscan missionary named Francisco Tomas Garces attempted to blaze a trail between the Spanish missions in California and the missions along the Rio Grande. His journey led him up the Colorado River into western Grand Canyon, where he encountered the Havasupai Indians. The Havasupai graciously invited Garces to stay for five days of feasting, an offer that he gladly accepted. When the five days were up, he set out to visit the Hopi villages to the east. But the Hopi, stung by years of warfare, were deeply suspicious of the Spaniard. They refused to feed Garces or even accept his gifts. Taking the hint, Garces returned to Havasu Canyon, where he was greeted with yet another multi-day feast.

Not long after Garces journey, another Spanish expedition, the Dominguez-Escalante party, left New Mexico to find a northern route to the Pacific. But by the time they reached the Sierra Nevada Mountains, winter's deep snows had already set in and the mountains were impassable. Forced to abandon their mission, the Spaniards headed south, at one point crossing the Colorado River near the present site of Lees Ferry at the northern tip of Grand Canyon. They were the third and final Spanish expedition to set eyes on Grand Canyon.

Although the Spanish had relatively little contact with Indians living in and around Grand Canyon, their indirect presence had a huge impact on Indian life. The Spanish introduced horses, cattle and sheep to North America—animals that would ultimately define many Southwestern tribes—as well as new fruits such as peaches, melons and figs. But along with these positive influences came many deadly diseases such as smallpox, which had a devastating impact on Indian populations throughout the Southwest.

Indian Pueblo

AMERICAN EXPLORERS

IN 1821 MEXICO gained independence from Spain and acquired much of the American Southwest. But Mexico, like Spain, generally avoided the desolate landscape, and Indians living near Grand Canyon remained relatively undisturbed. But a new power was looming on the eastern horizon.

Following the Louisiana Purchase in 1803, American beaver trappers began fanning out across the West. Before long they were scouring the streams that tumbled down from the Rockies and into the Four Corners region. But even then, Grand Canyon was generally avoided as a destination. Although beavers lived at the bottom of the Canyon, reaching them proved too arduous a task.

Not that some trappers didn't try. In 1826 a trapping party led by Ewing Young traveled up the Colorado River on foot to become the first Americans to set eyes on Grand Canyon. Their journey was a miserable one. At one point the men plodded through 18 inches of snow and ate bark to fend off starvation. Not surprisingly, they found little to like about the region. As one of the trappers, James Pattie, remembered, "We arrived where the river emerges from these horrid mountains, which so cage it up, as to deprive all human beings of the ability to descend to its banks, and make use of its waters."

Such descriptions did little to encourage further exploration. With its extreme climate, physically challenging terrain, and striking lack of water, the Four Corners region was a terrible place to settle—which was precisely why Mormon leader Brigham Young decided to settle there.

THE ILL-FATED EXPLORER

IN 1857 THE U.S. War Department authorized an expedition to explore the lower reaches of the Colorado River, led by novice Lieutenant Joseph Ives. Unfortunately for Ives, the expedition's 50-foot steamboat, *The Explorer*, was poorly designed to handle the rapids, shallows and sand bars of the Colorado. The boat ran aground countless times and the crew was often forced to unload and tow the boat by hand. After two months of slow progress and much towing, *The Explorer* struck a boulder near the present site of Hoover Dam. The crew was tossed overboard and the boat was wrecked beyond repair.

Defeated, Ives declared that he had reached the furthest point of navigation on the river. But not only was his declaration inaccurate, Ives had already been proven wrong. Several weeks earlier a man named George Johnson, incensed at being passed over by the War Department to lead the historic journey, steamed his own boat past the point where *The Explorer* wrecked.

Ives' expedition produced several fine maps of the region, but much of the Colorado remained as mysterious as ever. Writing in his log, Ives concluded his journey with the unfortunate remark: "The region is, of course, altogether valueless. It can be approached only from the south, and after entering it there is nothing to do but leave. Ours has been the first, and will doubtless be the last, party of whites to visit this profitless locality."

Today Grand Canyon, Hoover Dam, and nearby Las Vegas attract over 40 million visitors each year.

Fleeing religious persecution in Illinois, Young led his followers to Utah's Great Salt Lake in 1847. The harsh landscape offered the perfect refuge for the Mormons—a place where they could practice their new religion in peace. Over the next two decades, Mormon settlements spread south, representing the first significant white presence anywhere near Grand Canyon. But even the notoriously rugged Mormons refused to explore Grand Canyon's treacherous depths. That job would fall to a 34-year-old geology professor named John Wesley Powell.

JOHN WESLEY POWELL

IN 1848, FOLLOWING the conclusion of the Mexican War, the United States acquired the vast chunk of land that would one day make up California, Nevada, Arizona, Utah, Colorado and New Mexico. But even in the 1860s, maps of the United States had a single word splashed across the Grand Canyon region: UNEXPLORED. Most men, even the heroically rugged trappers who had opened up much of the West, took one look at those maps and stayed away. But one man looked at the maps and saw an opportunity for everlasting fame.

John Wesley Powell was probably the least likely man in America to conquer the Colorado River. A one-armed college professor with virtually no whitewater experience, he was a case study in everything that *wasn't* needed to successfully navigate the river. At five feet six inches tall he hardly cut an imposing figure. But what Powell lacked in physical stature, he more than made up for in personal ambition.

In 1868 Powell decided to organize an expedition to explore the Colorado River and the desolate canyon country it flowed through. He went to Washington, D.C. to raise money for the trip, but with the federal treasury still reeling from the Civil War government funds were hard to come by. Powell was offered some military

HERO or LIAR?

JAMES WHITE

IN 1867, two years before Powell's expedition, a raft was pulled from the Colorado River just below Grand Canyon. On board was a starving, sunburned, half-naked man named James White, who proceeded to tell a story so amazing it is still disputed to this day. White claimed to have spent the previous two weeks floating down the Colorado lashed to a raft, making him the first man to successfully run Grand Canyon. Most modern scholars dispute White's story, based primarily on the fact that it's so hard to believe. But supposing it's true, White's journey would have been one of the most remarkable whitewater adventures of all time rations, however, which he gladly accepted. Undaunted, he ultimately managed to scrape together funding from a variety of private institutions.

Powell's next step was to assemble a crew. The job offered no pay, harsh living conditions, and life-threatening risks. Not surprisingly, the men who accepted these terms were reckless, crazy or a little of both. Most were trappers and mountain men eager for adventure and excitement. But to Powell, the journey was primarily a scientific expedition. "The object," he wrote, "is to make collections in geology, natural history, antiquities, and ethnology."

On May 24, 1869, Powell's expedition launched four boats from Green River City, Wyoming. Their starting point was 6,100 feet above sea level. Their destination—Grand Wash Cliffs, near present-day Lake Mead—lay at an elevation of 1,300 feet. How the river got there was anybody's guess.

For the first week of their journey the men floated peacefully down the Green River. The one-armed Powell, unable to row, sat perched on a chair tied to his boat. At first the lazy current bored the men, but soon the river started to intensify. As they continued downstream, the rapids became frequent and fierce. On June 9, one of the boats slipped into a large rapid before the crew could scout it. The boat smashed on a rock and splintered into pieces. The three men onboard managed to swim to safety, but a third of the expedition's supplies were lost.

Following Disaster Falls (as Powell later named it) a nervous energy settled over the crew. They were only two weeks into their journey, and they had already

rescue by UNDERWEAR!

IN DESOLATION Canyon, Powell and a crew member named George Bradley set out to climb the steep cliffs above the river. As the one-armed Powell neared the top he became stranded on the edge of a cliff. "Standing on my toes my muscles began to tremble," he wrote. "If I lose my hold I shall fall to the bottom." Powell called to Bradley, who quickly appeared on a ledge above. With time running out, Bradley stripped off his long johns and lowered them down. But they dangled behind Powell just out of reach. Taking a deep breath, Powell leaned back into space and grabbed for the long johns with his one good hand. Catching a pant leg he held on for dear life while Bradley hauled him up to safety.

Disaster Falls

Powell expedition boats

lost one of their boats. What would happen if they lost another? The rapids were growing worse, and soon they would be hundreds of miles from civilization.

Determined, the men carried on. For the next two months they followed the Green River as it passed through Wyoming and Utah, running rapids whenever they could but spending most of their time lining or portaging. Lining involved guiding the boats downstream as the men held on to ropes from the shore. It was excruciating work. The ropes burned the men's hands and they were constantly slipping on wet rocks. The alternative was portaging, which entailed carrying the boats—and several thousand pounds of supplies—past the rapid on shore.

By the time the expedition reached the confluence of the Green River and the Grand River (the official start of the Colorado), supplies were running low. They were down to several pounds of spoiled bacon, a few sacks of flour, and some dried apples. The men tried to supplement their diet by hunting, but game in the region was scarce. Before long, the constant hunger and backbreaking days were taking a serious toll on group morale.

On August 4 the expedition reached the start of Grand Canyon. Drifting through the Canyon's upper reaches, Powell was spellbound by the variety of rocks he saw. He thought the highly polished limestone looked like marble, so he named this initial stretch Marble Canyon. Soon the cliffs rose up thousands of feet on either side. The scale of the canyon was breathtaking. "We are three quarters of a mile in the depths of the Earth," Powell wrote, "and the great river shrinks into insignificance, as it dashes its angry waves against the walls and cliffs, that rise to the world above; they are but puny ripples, and we are but pygmies."

While Powell marveled at the natural spectacle, many of the crew felt confined. The canyon was like a prison to them. Daytime highs topped 100°F and the rapids were frequent and fierce. Many began to openly regret their decision to come.

Continuing on, the men twisted deep in the heart of the Canyon. Soon they were fighting off rapids the size of three-story buildings. Even worse, they had no idea what to expect around each bend in the river. There were rumors of giant waterfalls deep in Grand Canyon, and if those rumors proved true the expedition would find itself trapped at the bottom of a mile deep chasm. Physically and mentally, the men were starting to unwind. They were now down to starvation rations, and the threat of death was very real.

On August 27 the men were camped above their worst rapid yet. Many in the group doubted they could run it and survive. That night at dinner, a man named Oramel Howland took Powell aside. Howland told Powell that he and two others were abandoning the expedition. They would take their chances climbing out of the canyon—a decision that carried equally lethal implications.

Powell respected their decision, but he was convinced the rapid could be run. And according to his calculations, the group was no more than 50 miles from the end of their journey. He spent all night trying to convince the men not to leave, but they had seen enough. The three men left the following morning. They were never seen again.

Concentrating on the matter at hand, Powell studied the rapid. The river was hemmed in by steep cliffs, so there was no possibility of portaging. And other than a small section at the top of the rapid, lining was also out of the question. With a slimmed down crew the men abandoned one of the boats and lined the remaining two boats as far as they could. Then they swooped down into the rapid.

The first boat rushed down a steep wave and was swamped with water. The men pulled for their lives. Soon the waves grew too large to do anything but hold on tight. The boats tossed and turned but somehow they managed to stay upright. Before the men knew it, the rapid was behind them. Both boats had survived.

Two days later, Powell's expedition reached the end of its journey. As they approached the confluence of the Colorado and the Virgin River, the men spotted several Mormons fishing in the river. The Mormons had been posted there for weeks, under orders from Brigham Young to keep their eyes out "for any fragments or relics of [Powell's] party that might drift down the stream." They were shocked to see Powell and his men alive.

The hearts of the skeletal river runners were filled with joy. The Mormons cooked them a meal, and as one crew member recalled, "we laid our dignified manners aside and assumed the manner of so many hogs. Ate as long as we could and went to sleep to wake up hungry." After 99 days on the river, their voyage was finally over.

Powell's death-defying expedition is virtually impossible to imagine today. River guides who have spent decades rowing the modern, dam-controlled Colorado simply shake their heads when they try to imagine Powell's historic trip. His under-supplied, ragtag collection of mountain men conquered the wildest, most unpredictable river in North America. Today, their journey is often referred to the last great expedition of the American West.

John Wesley Powell

John Wesley Powell's Colorado River expedition was one of the greatest adventures in American history. But nearly as remarkable as the expedition is the man who inspired it all.

John Wesley Powell was born in 1834, the son of a poor itinerant preacher who moved his family across the frontier. Even as a young man Powell was constantly on the go, enrolling in several different colleges but never staying around long enough to graduate from any of them. When the Civil War broke out, Powell enlisted on the Union side, making Lieutenant within his first two months. At the battle of Shiloh he was shot in his right arm—an injury that required amputation. Refusing to be kept out of the fight, Powell returned to action several months later and accompanied General Sherman on his conquest of Georgia.

Following the war, Powell underwent an operation to ease the constant pain in his amputated arm. The operation failed, and for the rest of his life Powell was plagued with chronic pain from the raw nerve endings at the end of his stump. Not one to dwell on personal misfortune, Powell simply looked to the future as he tried to figure out what to do with his life. "You are a maimed man," his father told him, "Settle down at teaching. It is a noble profession. Get this nonsense of science and adventure out of your mind."

Powell tried to settle down at teaching, but the lure of the West proved too powerful. As a geologist he had led research trips to the headwaters of the Colorado and Green Rivers—two rivers whose waters ultimately flow through Grand Canyon. It was there that Powell developed an obsession with the Southwest. Powell the geologist was convinced that the canyons of the Colorado would give "the best geological section on the continent." Powell the adventurer desperately wanted to be the first to conquer the final frontier of the United States.

And conquer it he did. Following his Grand Canyon expedition Powell achieved international fame. On the lecture circuit he spoke to packed houses and stayed in the finest hotels. Later, he used his influence to help found the Bureau of American Ethnology and the U.S. Geological Survey.

Powell died in 1902. Shortly before his death, he made an unusual bet with his friend W.J. McGee, president of the National Geographic Society. Although physically smaller than McGee, Powell was convinced his brain was larger. To settle the dispute, the men left instructions to have their brains weighed following their deaths. At 1,488 grams, Powell's brain was five percent heavier. Today it rests in a jar at the Smithsonian Institute.

EARLY SETTLERS

POWELL'S JOURNEY INAUGURATED a wave of expeditions to map and explore the Grand Canyon. Leading this charge was John Wesley Powell himself. Shortly after his historic near-death, near-mutiny expedition, Powell announced plans to lead a second trip down the Colorado. Many of his scientific notes had been lost on the first journey, and he was determined to fill in the blanks. This time, however, he would break his trip into stages with supply points along the way, significantly reducing the risks involved. And so, in 1871, the indefatigable Powell conquered the Colorado yet again.

Between river trips Powell conducted scientific expeditions along the rim. But these excursions were only temporary. The region as a whole remained largely uninhabited. Following the arrival of the railroad in northern Arizona in the early 1880s, however, a handful of drifters started taking up permanent residence along the South Rim.

Most of these early settlers were miners who assumed Grand Canyon hid vast mineral riches. Although a number of potential mining sites were located, the costs of excavation soon proved prohibitively expensive. Ore had to be packed out on burros, water was scarce, and the closest railroad lay two days away. Mining the Grand Canyon, it tuned out, was an extremely unprofitable endeavor. But just as that realization started to sink in, the miners discovered another source of revenue: tourists.

Starting in the mid-1880s, people began arriving at the Grand Canyon for no other reason than to visit, relax, and take in the views. This was a strikingly new concept. For hundreds of years the Grand Canyon had been avoided—even detested—as a destination. Now, people thought it was beautiful. It was an idea that would turn out to be highly contagious.

The first tourists arrived at the South Rim in 1884. They stayed in make-shift lodges built by miners. Most visitors arrived by stagecoach from the nearby towns of Flagstaff, Williams, and Ash Fork, but the journey was a rugged one. The dirt roads were filled with potholes, and the trip often required at least two days of bone-jarring travel.

It wasn't long before people began looking for a better form of transportation to the rim. In 1885 Bill Bass brought a railroad agent to his lodge to try to convince him of the potential of a spur line to Grand Canyon. The agent was hardly impressed. "No one," he wrote to his superiors, "would go that far only to see a hole in the ground."

It would take over a decade for the railroads to realize their mistake. When they finally did, the previously isolated Grand Canyon would find itself linked directly to the modern world, and visitors would arrive by the thousands.

GRAND CANYON PIONEERS

JOHN HANCE

JOHN HANCE was the first permanent white settler in Grand Canyon. He came on a prospecting trip in 1881 and immediately fell in love with the scenery. Two years later, he built a log cabin east of Grandview Point and started renting out rooms to guests.

Hance is fondly remembered as Grand Canyon's premier storyteller, but his stories rarely contained a shred of truth. He took great pleasure in spinning tall tales with a deadpan delivery until his hapless listeners realized they'd been had. One of his favorite stories involved the time the Grand Canyon filled with clouds. According to Hance, he walked across the clouds on snowshoes, but became stranded on a pinnacle when the clouds started to clear. Another time he jumped across the entire canyon on horseback. Hance had hundreds of stories in his repertoire, and he never told the same story twice in exactly the same way.

As Hance once confided to a friend, "I've got to tell stories to them people for their money; and if I don't tell it to them, who will? I can make these tenderfeet believe that a frog eats boiled eggs; and I'm going to do it; and I'm going to make 'em believe that he carries it a mile to find a rock to crack it on."

The tenderfeet loved it. According to one early visitor, "Anyone who comes to the Grand Canyon and fails to meet John Hance will miss half the show." In 1906 he was offered free room and board at the Bright Angel Lodge in exchange for just hanging out with the guests and being himself.

JOHN D. LEE

BEFORE HE was banished to the Grand Canyon by Brigham Young, John D. Lee had been a prosperous Mormon living in southern Utah with his 19 wives. But in 1857 Lee participated in the Mountain Meadow Massacre, in which a group of Mormons slaughtered a wagon train of 120 pioneers on their way to California. In a blatant cover up, the Mormon Church placed the blame solely on Lee's shoulders. With the law at his back, Lee fled to Grand Canyon.

Lee arrived at a place along the Colorado River just south of present-day Lake Powell. There he established Lees Ferry. It was the only viable river crossing for hundreds of miles. But being a wanted man and owning one of the only ferry crossings for hundreds of miles turned out to be a dangerous combination. In 1874 the law finally caught up with Lee, and he was tried and executed. He was survived by his 53 children.

BILL BASS

BILL BASS moved to Williams, Arizona from New Jersey in 1883. Several years later, curiosity and prospecting brought him to the South Rim, where he spent the next 41 years of his life.

Bass came to Grand Canyon to prospect, but he soon turned to tourism as his main source of income. He built a crude tent camp along the South Rim, which he promoted through home-made lantern slides that were displayed throughout the country.

In 1894 Bass guided a young woman named Ada Diefendorf to the beautiful waterfalls in Havasu Canyon. A short while later the two were married, and Ada became the first white woman to raise a family on the South Rim. But life in Grand Canyon was never easy. In addition to household duties such as cooking and cleaning, Ada had to wrangle horses, care for livestock, and hike three days to do laundry in the Colorado River.

In 1926, at the age of 77, Bass sold the claims to his land holdings and retired to Wickenburg, Arizona. By the time he left, he had built more roads and inner-canyon trails than any other individual in Grand Canyon history.

282

THE RAILROAD ARRIVES

MINERS AT THE rim weren't the only ones interested in a railroad to Grand Canyon. The nearby towns of Flagstaff and Williams also realized the benefits that a railroad would bring—namely increased tourist dollars—and both towns were soon engaged in a feverish competition to build one. Flagstaff envisioned a railroad supported by tourism. The town's leading citizens pitched their idea to a number of established railroad companies, but as Bill Bass had already discovered, the railroads failed to grasp Grand Canyon's tourist potential.

Williams took a different approach. It appealed to the mining companies who needed a cheap way to haul ore from mines located just south of the canyon. Mining operations would be the driving force of the new railroad, with tourist dollars providing additional revenue. It was a shrewd pitch, and in 1897 the Santa Fe and Grand Canyon Railway Company was incorporated to build a railroad connecting Williams to the South Rim.

Four years later, the Santa Fe Railroad reached Grand Canyon Village. By that time, however, the mines that spearheaded its creation had already shut down. It hardly mattered. For $3.95 passengers could now enjoy a smooth, four-hour ride to the South Rim (as opposed to the $20, bouncing, all-day stage ride that was previously the only option). The result was predictable: tourism boomed.

Visitors arrived by the thousands. The railroad flourished, and before long land near Grand Canyon Village had become one of the most desirable commodities in the region. A few cunning locals began staking bogus mining claims along the South Rim, giving them the questionable right to develop the land. Although the practice was ultimately ruled illegal, a few citizens—most notably Ralph Cameron (p.96)—became very rich off the scheme.

Bogus mining claims aside, the Santa Fe Railroad still owned most of the land surrounding its tracks, giving it a strategic advantage in the local real estate game. To accommodate the flood of new visitors, it built an extravagant new hotel—El Tovar—in Grand Canyon Village in 1905. Early settlers who built hotels away from Grand Canyon Village soon found it hard to compete. Within a decade, most locally owned hotels had shut down.

Life on the rim was changing fast. Just three months after the first train pulled up to the South Rim, the first automobile arrived. Its driver had departed from Flagstaff several days earlier amid much fanfare, but the car broke down soon after it left. Several days later the automobile arrived at the South Rim pulled by a team of mules. The trip was hardly a bad omen. Within two and a half decades automobiles would become the most popular form of transportation to Grand Canyon, ultimately forcing the railroad out of business.

While the South Rim was buzzing with tourist activity, the North Rim remained as isolated as ever. No railroads came within 100 miles of the North Rim, and settlement was scare. Because of its extreme isolation, the Arizona Strip—the narrow stretch of land between the North Rim and Utah—was a lawless area that attracted a strange mix of cattle thieves, renegades, and Mormons who continued to practice polygamy. (The Arizona Strip continues to attract a similar mix of renegades to this day). Although Utah tried several times to annex the Arizona Strip, citing Arizona's poor law enforcement as a primary concern, Arizona was able to retain control of the land.

Because of its remote location, the North Rim was flush with wild game, a fact that soon attracted hunting parties. Sport hunting on the North Rim got off to a rocky start in 1892 when a man named John Young came up with the idea of building a hunting lodge that would cater to British aristocrats. Young contacted Buffalo Bill Cody, who was performing in England at the time, and convinced him to round up a group of potential British investors. The eager Britons arrived later that year, took one look at the desolate landscape, and hightailed it back to England.

American hunters, on the other hand, were more than happy to venture to the rugged North Rim, and sport hunting flourished. In 1906 Congress established Grand Canyon Game Reserve, which included much of the North Rim. A few years later ex-President Theodore Roosevelt visited the North Rim on a hunting trip. Starting from the South Rim, he descended the Bright Angel trail and boarded a metal cage that shuttled passengers across the river via a cable and pulley system. Halfway across the river, one of the cables snapped. The cage jolted, but it was still in working order. Once safely across, the President cried out, "Let's do it again!"

High-profile visits like these focused even greater attention on Grand Canyon. It soon became clear that the region was not just a fly-by-night tourist destination, but a major national landmark. Many felt that it deserved to be recognized as such. Before long, the wheels were in motion to create Grand Canyon National Park.

the LION HUNTER

IN 1906 James "Uncle Jim" Owens was appointed manager of the newly established Grand Canyon Game Reserve. Although game was now legally protected in Grand Canyon, the definition of game did not apply to predators such as bobcats and mountain lions. In fact, these animals were aggressively hunted to protect other, "less threatening" game. During his time on the North Rim, Uncle Jim claimed to have shot over 1,200 mountain lions. Others put that number closer to 550. Regardless, the walls of his cabin were covered with mountain lion claws and a sign outside advertised, "Lions Caught to Order, Reasonable Rates." It wasn't until several decades later that predator hunting was finally banned in Grand Canyon.

the south rim SWINDLER

Of ALL THE real estate swindlers who came to Grand Canyon, none was more successful than Ralph Cameron. Shortly after the arrival of the railroad, Cameron began staking mining claims along the South Rim. Before long he had staked over 13,000 acres. But Cameron had little interest in mining. The claims gave him the right to develop the land, which was much more valuable as commercial real estate.

For his claims to be legal, however, he needed to actually mine the land. Cameron paid little attention to this technicality. He simply "salted" the claims with imported minerals and set up bogus mining equipment. Once his claims were established, Cameron took great pleasure in lording them over the Santa Fe Railroad, who felt *they* had the right to develop the land.

One of Cameron's most contentious claims was located next to the train depot, a spot where he knew the railroad wanted to build a hotel. Cameron built his own hotel there instead. In retaliation, the railroad moved their terminal several hundred feet to the east so train passengers would have to pass the railroad-owned Bright Angel Hotel on their way to Cameron's hotel. Visitation at Cameron's hotel plummeted.

But Cameron had one more trick up his sleeve. His claims also gave him sole control of the Bright Angel Trail, the only trail into the canyon anywhere near Grand Canyon Village, and Cameron charged $1 a head for every tourist who wanted to descend the trail on horseback. The railroad filed a lawsuit, but Cameron prevailed in court. This time, the railroad went on the offensive, spending thousands of dollars improving the Hermit Trail, located several miles west of the Bright Angel Trail. But Cameron owned mining claims there too, and he howled at the injustice. Tired of his antics, the railroad relented and paid him $40,000 for his bogus claims.

As the years wore on, Cameron lost the will to compete with the railroad. In 1910 he shut down his hotel, but he continued to charge a toll on the Bright Angel Trail. By the time the Park Service finally gained control of the trail, Cameron had leveraged his wealth and power into a seat in the U.S. Senate. For years he continued to fight the park over the legitimacy of his mining claims. It wasn't until 1920 that the Arizona Supreme Court finally invalidated his claims, ending his once-grand real estate empire.

Grand Canyon
Santa Fe
of Arizona
The California Limited
- the train of luxury -
takes you to the rim of this world-wonder
u may stop at El Tovar Hotel, managed by Fred Harvey
May I send you our art booklets
describing the Canyon and the Limited?
Free on request. Address W. J. Black, Pass Traffic Mgr. A.T.& S.F. Ry. System
1119 Z Railway Exchange Chicago

John Hance & Teddy Roosevelt

Park Entrance, 1931

GRAND CANYON NATIONAL PARK

BY THE LATE 1800s, the wheels were in motion to create Grand Canyon National Park. As early as 1886 Indiana Senator Benjamin Harrison had introduced legislation to preserve Grand Canyon as a national park. At that time there was only one other national park—Yellowstone, created in 1872—and Harrison's legislation sputtered out due to lack of enthusiasm. Two decades later, when Harrison was President, he used his power to establish "Great Canyon Reserve." It was a victory for Grand Canyon, but many Arizona miners and cattlemen resented the new restrictions placed on the land. They would ultimately provide some of the most vocal opposition to the creation of a national park.

Despite scattered local opposition, there were many who saw the need to protect Grand Canyon. In 1906 the Act for the Preservation of American Antiquities was passed, giving the President the power to set aside areas that held "objects of historic or scientific nature." That same year President Theodore Roosevelt created Grand Canyon Game Reserve. For Roosevelt it was an easy decision. He had visited the Grand Canyon a few years earlier and proclaimed it to be "the most impressive scenery I have ever looked at."

The creation of Grand Canyon Game Reserve was just the beginning. In 1908, Roosevelt established Grand Canyon National Monument, the highest designation a piece of American land can receive without Congressional approval. At that point Arizona was not yet a state, and it had no Senators or Congressmen to champion the creation of a national park. Then, in 1912, Arizona was admitted to the Union.

In 1917 Representative Carl Hayden and Senator Henry Fountain of Arizona introduced legislation to create Grand Canyon National Park. On February 26, 1919 President Woodrow Wilson signed the bill into law.

But creating a national park and running it smoothly were two different matters. Early administration officials lacked a coherent vision for the park, and many major infrastructure issues went unresolved. In its first decade of operation Grand Canyon National Park went through six superintendents. The park needed a strong leader with a long-term commitment to Grand Canyon. It found that leader in Miner Tillotson, a civil engineer who became superintendent in 1927 and occupied the position for over a decade. Through his tireless efforts he helped shape a coherent administrative vision of the park that set the precedent for years to come.

The same year that Tillotson became superintendent, Congress revised the park's boundaries to include a large portion of Kaibab National Forest. Five years later President Herbert Hoover proclaimed a new Grand Canyon National Monument (the old one had become Grand Canyon National Park) that encompassed 300 square miles in western Grand Canyon and an additional 40 miles along the Colorado River.

The park was a success on paper, but the flood of new visitors soon overwhelmed the staff. In its first year as a National Park, Grand Canyon received 44,000 visitors. Within a decade, that number had increased to nearly 200,000. In 1937, 300,000 arrived. The numbers kept climbing, but the park's staff remained the same—10 rangers and one park superintendent. It is a testament to the dedication of these early National Park Service employees that such a small staff was able to accommodate so many people. Ultimately, the number of rangers was increased, making the park much more enjoyable for visitors and employees alike.

THE GREAT DAM WARS

BY THE 1960s Grand Canyon seemed to be doing just fine. Its dedicated staff was welcoming millions of people from around the world. Movie stars, British royalty, and Arab sheiks all stopped by for a look. The giant hole in the ground that had been avoided for centuries was now one of the nation's most cherished natural landmarks. Best of all, its national park status protected the land from private development. But a massive government project soon threatened to drastically alter the landscape.

In the early 1960s the U.S. Bureau of Reclamation (the government agency responsible for much of the West's water supply) went looking for a new place to build a dam. Ever since the overwhelming success of Hoover Dam, the Bureau had been building dams at a frantic rate. The West was growing fast, and it needed water to grow, so in the 1930s, '40s and '50s the Bureau of Reclamation built dams wherever it could. It created huge reservoirs—some the size of small eastern states—that trapped water flowing out to sea. Before long, many of the Southwest's most impressive rivers resembled a string of interconnected reservoirs. By the early 1960s there was only one good place left in America to build a giant dam: Grand Canyon.

With its steep walls, deep side canyons, and powerful river, Grand Canyon was the perfect site for a dam. But there was a catch: any reservoir created by a dam would be totally impractical from a water-use standpoint. The water would have to be pumped out thousands of feet to bring it to civilization, and the costs involved would be prohibitively expensive. But the Bureau of Reclamation wasn't interested in water. It was interested in hydroelectricity. In effect, a dam in Grand Canyon would be nothing more than a giant cash register to fund other, less economically feasible water projects elsewhere. And the Bureau of Reclamation didn't just want one dam in the Grand Canyon. It wanted two.

When conservationists heard the news they went wild. Conservationists hate dams, a fact that became glaringly apparent in 1948 when the Bureau of Reclamation tried to build a dam along the Green River in Echo Park, Utah. The dam would have flooded part of Dinosaur National Monument, and conservationists were loath to let that happen. Led by David Brower of the Sierra Club, they fought tooth and nail to defeat the dam. They succeeded. But their success came at a huge cost.

As part of the compromise to save Dinosaur National Monument, the two sides agreed upon a new dam farther downstream. The site of the new dam would be Glen Canyon. Lying just north of Grand Canyon, Glen Canyon was one of the most remote places in the country. Only a few thousand people had ever set eyes upon it. So shortly before Glen Canyon Dam was finished, David Brower, the man who had been instrumental in its creation, took a river trip through Glen Canyon to see it for himself. He immediately started to cry.

With its gorgeous sandstone arches, fern covered alcoves, and sweeping river views, Glen Canyon was one of the most beautiful places Brower had ever seen. In a few months it would all be underwater. Brower would later admit that the

FLOYD DOMINY

"I like Dave Brower, but I don't think he's the sanctified conservationist that so many people think he is. I think he's a selfish preservationist, for the few. Dave Brower hates my guts. Why? Because I've got guts. I've tangled with Dave Brower for many years."

creation of Glen Canyon Dam was the greatest failure of his life. From that moment on, he vowed never again to lose another beautiful place to a dam. When he found out that the Bureau of Reclamation wanted to build two more dams in the Grand Canyon, he went into overdrive.

Brower was up against stiff competition. The biggest proponent of the new dams was the head of the Bureau of Reclamation, a man named Floyd Dominy. Dominy had spent his early years helping struggling Wyoming ranchers build dams to save their families from poverty. He knew firsthand how a lack of water could lead to suffering, and he made it his life's mission to build dams. Dominy's drive and ambition were unprecedented. By the time he became head of the Bureau of Reclamation he had many powerful allies, including Arizona Senator Carl Hayden, the chairman of the Appropriations Committee.

Brower versus Dominy. Conservation versus economic growth. The battle over the dams in Grand Canyon soon became much more than a battle for Grand Canyon. It became a battle for the future of environmental policy in America. For decades economic development had taken precedent over wilderness. But wilderness was disappearing fast, and many people wanted to preserve what was left before it was too late.

Debate over the dams soon shifted into the public arena. Defending the proposed dams, the Bureau of Reclamation argued that the reservoirs would help tourists enjoy Grand Canyon more fully by allowing them to explore previously inaccessible reaches of the Canyon from motorboats. In response, the Sierra Club took out full-page ads in the *New York Times*, *Los Angeles Times*, *San Francisco Chronicle*, and *Washington Post*. The ads read: "Should we also flood the Sistine Chapel so tourists can get nearer the ceiling?"

The response was overwhelming. Letters protesting the dams arrived at the Bureau of Reclamation in dump trucks. Senators and Congressmen were flooded with requests to save Grand Canyon. The two dams, which would have flooded much of Marble Canyon and the Lower Granite Gorge (including Havasu Creek, one of the most beautiful place in the canyon), were stopped dead in their tracks.

DAVID BROWER

"Lake Powell is a drag strip for power boats. It's for people who won't do things except the easy way. The magic of Glen Canyon is dead. It has been vulgarized. Putting water in the Cathedral in the Desert was like urinating on the crypt of St. Peter's."

GRAND CANYON TODAY

TODAY THE BIGGEST challenge facing Grand Canyon is the park's overwhelming number of visitors. In 1956 one million people visited Grand Canyon. Thirteen years later that number doubled. Twenty years later it tripled. To cope with increased traffic and pollution, the park service closed Hermit Road to private vehicles in 1974 and began and offering a free shuttle instead. To deal with overcrowding below the rim, the park instituted a permit and reservation system for overnight camping; before the permit system it was not unusual for hundreds of people to camp at the bottom of the Canyon near Phantom Ranch, a place that can accommodate about 90 people comfortably.

To cope with increasing visitation in the future, the National Park Service has drafted a General Management Plan to reduce human impact on the park and keep Grand Canyon in as natural a state as possible. Under the plan, which will be instituted over time, private cars will not be allowed over much of the South Rim and visitors will be shuttled around entirely by bus or a proposed light rail system. Extensive "greenway trails" along the rim are also being built for bikers and pedestrians.

Today over four million people visit Grand Canyon each year. Those numbers are both a blessing and a challenge. But as long as every visitor makes a conscious effort to appreciate and preserve the Grand Canyon, it will remain one of the world's great destinations for generations to come.

OARS
DORIES

THE SOUTH RIM

THE SOUTH RIM

THE SOUTH RIM, located about 80 miles north of Flagstaff, is what most people think of when they think of Grand Canyon. Here you'll find the park's most famous sights and attractions, as well as the majority of the its lodges, campgrounds and restaurants.

Because of the South Rim's proximity to Interstate 40, which runs through Flagstaff and Williams, it's the most accessible part of the park—and therefore the most crowded. During peak summer weekends, some popular viewpoints can feel more like Times Square than the Great Outdoors. But no matter how crowded the South Rim gets, it's always worth it. The views are simply beyond compare.

The South Rim is divided into three main areas: Grand Canyon Village (p.122), Hermit Road (p.142), and Desert View Drive (p.156), all of which provide access to dramatic viewpoints and great hikes. To help reduce traffic, the park offers a free shuttle connecting lodges, park buildings, and popular viewpoints in Grand Canyon Village and along Hermit Road. If you want to explore Hermit Road, which offers some of the South Rim's finest viewpoints, you'll have to ride the shuttle between March 1 and November 30, when the road is closed to private vehicle traffic. You'll still need a car, however, to explore Desert View Drive, which heads 25 miles east of Grand Canyon Village to Desert View (p.168), a beautiful overlook in the Canyon's remote southeastern corner.

Grand Canyon Village is the hub of all tourist activity on the South Rim. Its five lodges—the only ones on the South Rim—accommodate about 1,000 guests, and nearby services including everything from fine dining to auto repair. Grand Canyon Village is also the jumping off point for narrated bus tours (p.118) and mule trips along popular trails (p.119), as well as the meeting spot for many of the park's excellent (and free) ranger programs (p.118).

Other than the easy Rim Trail (p.117), which skirts the edge of the Canyon in Grand Canyon Village and along Hermit Road, hiking on the South Rim is limited to a handful of trails that drop down the Canyon's steep walls to the Colorado River. Hiking from the rim to the river and back in a single day is *extremely* dangerous (some hikers have died in their attempts), but day hikers can still get a sense of the Inner Canyon's beauty by descending only partway down popular trails. The Bright Angel Trail (p.170) is the South Rim's most famous (and crowded) hike, but the Hermit Trail (p.184) and Grandview Trail (p.190) offer equally dramatic scenery with fewer crowds.

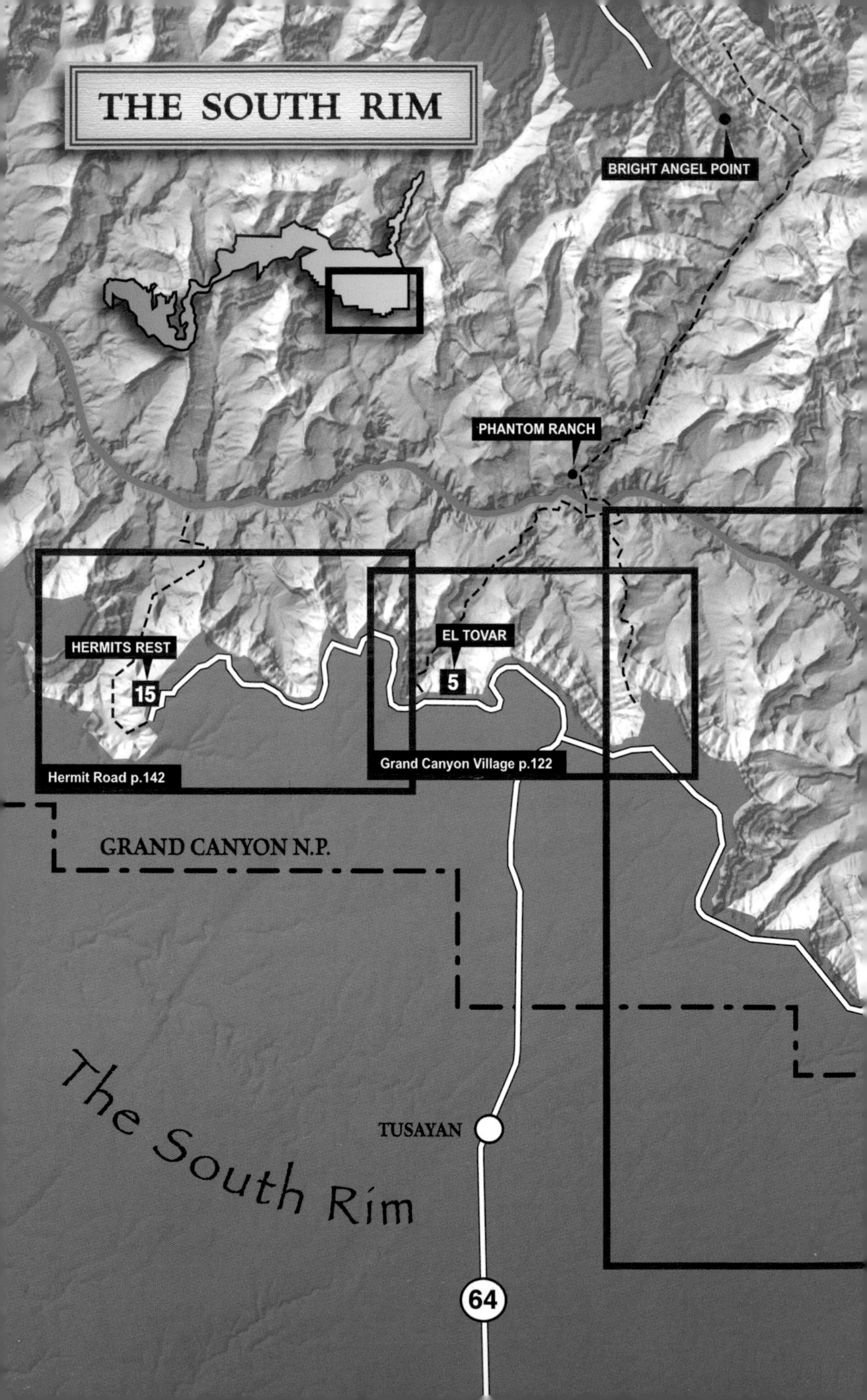
THE SOUTH RIM
BRIGHT ANGEL POINT
PHANTOM RANCH
HERMITS REST
15
EL TOVAR
5
Hermit Road p.142
Grand Canyon Village p.122
GRAND CANYON N.P.
TUSAYAN
64
The South Rim

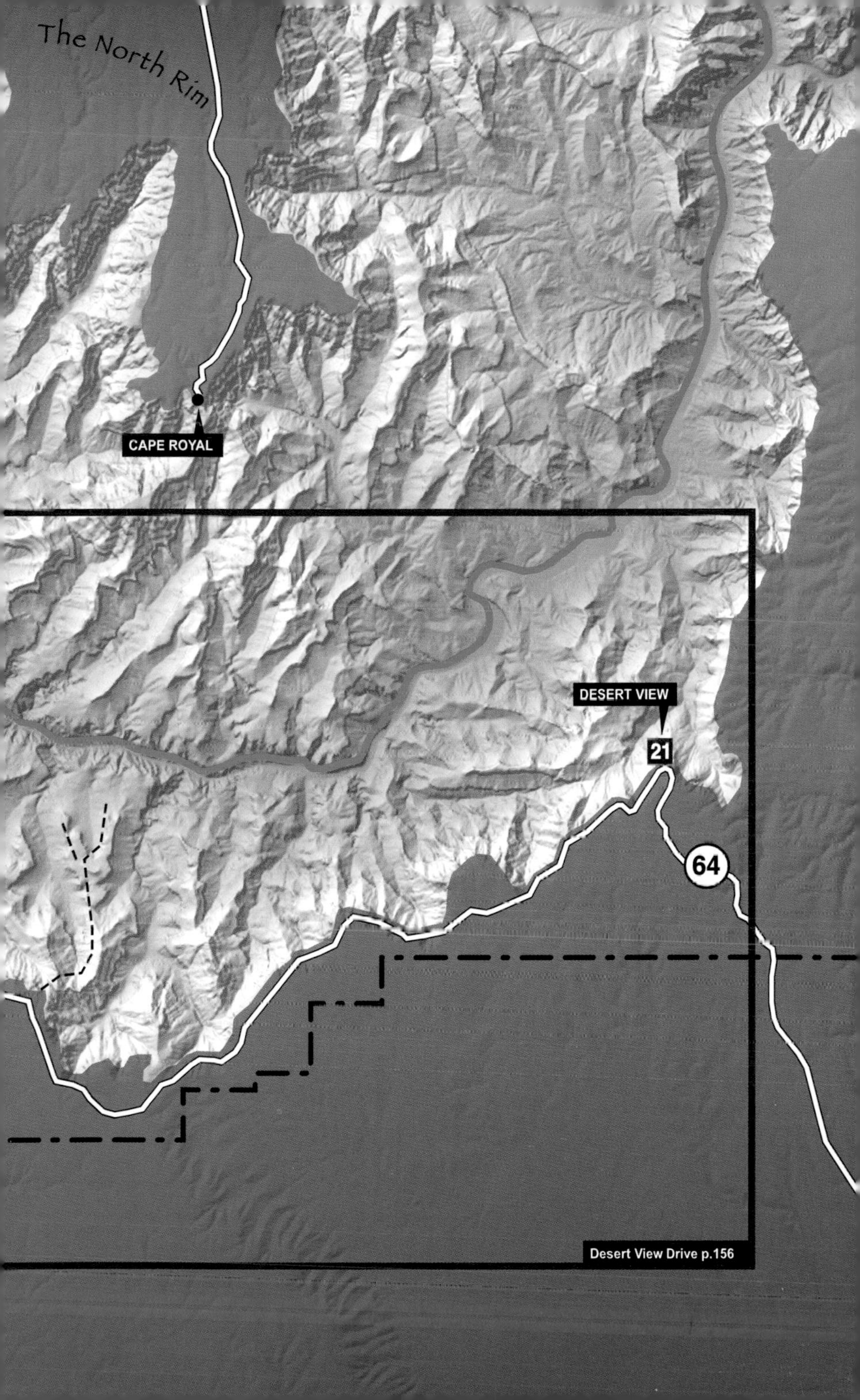
The North Rim
CAPE ROYAL
DESERT VIEW
21
64
Desert View Drive p.156

South Rim BASICS

GETTING TO THE SOUTH RIM

BY CAR

If you're traveling from Flagstaff or Williams, the most direct route to the South Rim heads north from I-80 on AZ–64, past the small towns of Valle and Tusayan, to Grand Canyon's South Entrance Station (about 60 miles total). From there it's a short drive to Grand Canyon Village. An alternate, slightly more scenic route from Flagstaff follows US–180 past the dramatic San Francisco Peaks to Valle, where US–180 merges with AZ-64.

If you're arriving from the northeast, your best bet is to enter the park via the eastern stretch of AZ–64. From US–89 follow AZ–64 to the East Entrance Station, about 25 miles east of Grand Canyon Village.

BY BUS

Greyhound (800-231-2222, www.greyhound.com) stops in Williams and Flagstaff.

Open Road Tours and Transportation (800-766-7117, www.openroadtours.com) offers shuttles from the Amtrak station in Flagstaff to Tusayan and Grand Canyon Village. Cost: $25 one-way. Shuttles from Phoenix to Flagstaff are also offered.

BY TRAIN

Amtrak (800-USA-RAIL, www.amtrak.com) runs trains to Williams and Flagstaff.

Grand Canyon Trailway (800-843-8724, www.thetrain.com) offers daily train service from Williams to Grand Canyon Village in vintage railroad cars, some of which are more luxurious (and expensive) than others. The ride lasts about two hours and features mock hold-ups and singing conductors. The train runs every day of the year except Christmas and Christmas Eve day. Cost: $70–$160.

BY PLANE

The two closest major airports to the South Rim are **McCarran Int'l Airport** in Las Vegas (702-261-5211, www.mccarran.com) and **Phoenix Sky Harbor Int'l Airport** (602-273-3300, www.phxskyharbor.com). Keep in mind that Phoenix is about 220 miles from the South Rim and Las Vegas is about 290 miles from the South Rim via major highways. Private planes and charter flights can fly to tiny **Grand Canyon Airport** in Tusayan.

INFORMATION

The best source of seasonal Grand Canyon information (shuttle times, ranger programs, etc.) is the park's free newspaper, *The Guide*. Copies of *The Guide* are available at all park entrance stations, visitor centers, and lodges. For answers to other questions, check out the ranger-staffed visitor center at Canyon View Information Plaza (p.126), or the information desks at Yavapai Observation Station (p.129), Kolb Studio (p.140), Tusayan Museum (p.165), or Desert View (p.168).

WHEN TO GO

The South Rim is open year-round. Summer is hands-down the most popular time to visit, but the massive crowds, hot temperatures, and frequent thunderstorms often combine to make this a less than ideal time to visit. Furthermore, scorching midday temperatures in the inner canyon can make many of the park's popular hiking trails unbearable in July and August. Despite these annoyances, the view from the rim remains spectacular (and many folks enjoy the dramatic scenery provided by a late-summer thunderstorm). Spring and fall, meanwhile, offer reduced crowds and much more manageable temperatures. Spring is also wildflower season, when explosions of color often appear below the rim. Finally there's winter, which brings freezing temperatures, minimal crowds, and reduced rates at park lodges. And if you're lucky enough to visit after the occasional dusting of snow, you'll witness Grand Canyon at its most beautiful.

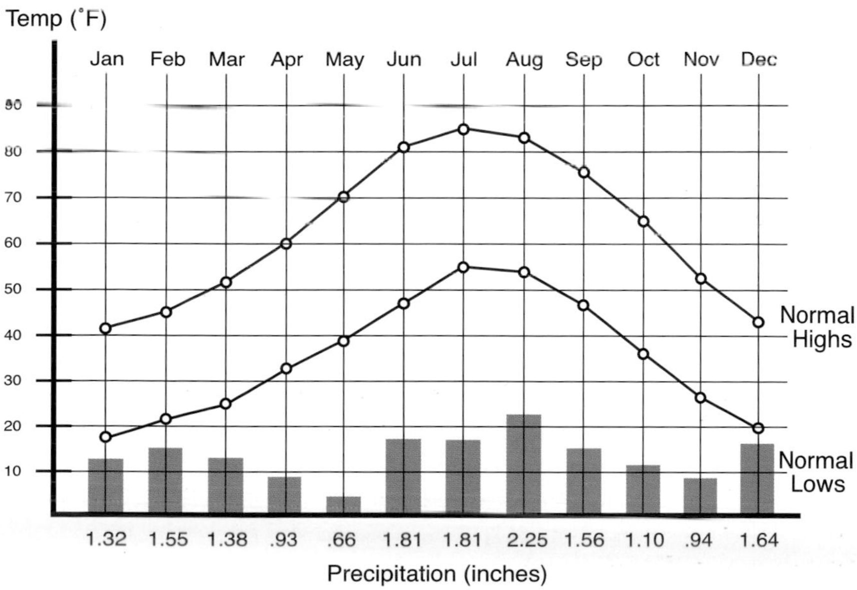

FEES

The entrance fee for the South Rim (which also gives you access to the North Rim) is $20 per vehicle or $10 per pedestrian, motorcycle rider, or cyclist. Admission is good for seven days. Another option is to purchase a $50 National Parks Pass (also available at the entrance station) that gives you unlimited access to all U.S. national parks and national monuments for one full year.

WEATHER

South Rim weather varies dramatically from season to season. Summer is hot, with daytime highs often topping 80°F, and short afternoon thundershowers sweep through Grand Canyon on a regular basis during monsoon season (July, August, and early September). Winter brings the occasional snowfall, but the snow that falls usually melts within a few days. Spring and fall, the best times to visit, boast less precipitation and milder temperatures than summer or winter.

WHAT TO BRING

Clothes: Even summer nights can get chilly on the South Rim, so be sure to pack warm clothes. Rain gear is also essential during monsoon season.

Supplies: Bring supplies for activities interest you (hiking, camping, etc.). If you happen to forget some basic supplies, there's a general store in Grand Canyon Village that carries a wide range of food, camping supplies, and other gear.

LODGING

Lodging in Grand Canyon is run by **Xanterra Parks and Resorts** (888-297-2757, www.grandcanyonlodges.com). Rooms fill up fast, so book your reservations as far in advance as possible, *especially* in the busy summer months. Xanterra accepts reservations up to 13 months in advance. Rates listed below are based on the busy summer season. Winter specials can be as much as $40 cheaper.

BRIGHT ANGEL LODGE

Located right on the rim of the canyon, this rustic hotel offers lodge rooms (no TV, some without private bath) and cabin rooms (TV, private bath). All rooms have telephones. The most popular room at Bright Angel Lodge is the Bucky O'Neill Suite ($240 per night), which has a working fireplace and two front doors that open directly onto the rim. See page 135 for more on Bright Angel Lodge.
Rates: Lodge and cabin rooms, $55; Cabins, $85–$130

EL TOVAR HOTEL

The finest lodge in the park, filled with historic elegance and rustic charm. El Tovar is located right on the rim, but just three of its 75 rooms offer sweeping views of the Canyon (although several more offer partial views). All rooms have full bathrooms, air conditioning, cable TV, and telephones. See page 132 for more.

Rates: $130–$300

KACHINA & THUNDERBIRD LODGES

These two identical modern buildings, set back about 60 feet from the rim, are situated between Bright Angel Lodge and El Tovar. Kachina and Thunderbird offer standard motel-style rooms with two queen beds, telephone, and full bath. Although some rooms face the canyon, there's little in the way of views. Note: Check in at Kachina Lodge is handled by the front desk at El Tovar; check in at Thunderbird Lodge is handled by the front desk at Bright Angel Lodge.

Rates: $125–$135

MASWIK LODGE

Set back 1/4 mile from the rim, Maswik Lodge offers motel-style rooms with two queen beds, a full bath, TV, and telephones. The lodge is divided into north and south sections (rooms in the north section are nicer and more expensive). In the summer rustic cabins with two double beds, shower, TV, and telephone are also offered. Couch potatoes will love Maswik Lodge's TV-filled sports bar.

Rates: South section, $80; North Section, $120; Rustic cabins, $75

PHANTOM RANCH

This collection of rustic buildings offers the only overnight lodging at the bottom of the canyon. Accessible by foot or mule via the Bright Angel Trail (p.170) or South Kaibab Trail (p.180), Phantom Ranch offers bunkhouses and private cabins that sleep up to four. (Most private cabins are reserved for mule riders on overnight trips, but two hikers cabin are available). Because all food it brought down by mule, meals *must* be reserved in advance. Due to its immense popularity, rooms should be reserved as far in advance as possible.

Rates: Bunkhouse, $30; Cabin, $75

YAVAPAI LODGE

The largest lodge in the park. Because Yavapai Lodge is situated 1/2 mile back from the rim, it's less popular than other lodges. But it's also the most likely to have rooms on short notice. All rooms have full bath, TV, and telephones. Some rooms have air conditioning.

Rates: $100–$110

CAMPING ON THE RIM

DESERT VIEW CAMPGROUND

This campground, located 26 miles east of Grand Canyon Village at Desert View (p.168), is open from mid-May through mid-October. Sites are available on a first-come, first-served basis. Each site accommodates up to six people, three tents, and two vehicles. No RV hook-ups. Cost: $10 per night.

MATHER CAMPGROUND

This large campground, located in Grand Canyon Village, offers year-round camping. Sites accommodate up to six people, three tents, and two vehicles. No RV hook-ups, 30-foot maximum vehicle length. Reservations can be made up to five months in advance and are strongly recommended December–March. Group sites accommodating up to 50 people are also available. For reservations visit www.reservations.nps.gov or call 800-365-2267. Cost: $15; Group sites, $40.

TRAILER VILLAGE

This RV campground, located next to Mather Campground and open year-round, offers RV hook-ups and accommodates vehicles up to 50 feet in length. Reservations are highly recommended April–October; contact Xanterra (888-297-2757, www.grandcanyonlodges.com). Call 928-638-2631 for same-day reservations. Cost: $25.

INNER CANYON CAMPING

Two popular campgrounds, accessible by foot or mule only, are located below the South Rim. Both have restrooms, running water, and emergency phones. Reservations (issued as permits by the Backcountry Office) are *essential*. See page 19 for more information on Backcountry Permits.

INDIAN GARDEN CAMPGROUND

Located 4.6 miles down the popular Bright Angel Trail (p.170), this campground sits above the lush banks of Garden Creek, which supports a thriving population of shady cottonwood trees.

BRIGHT ANGEL CAMPGROUND

A picture-perfect campground located at the bottom of the Canyon, not far from Phantom Ranch and the Colorado River. The campground is scattered along the banks of Bright Angel Creek. Each of thirty-two sites comes with a picnic table and fire ring. Bright Angel Campground is accessible via the Bright Angel Trail or South Kaibab Trail (p.178).

GETTING AROUND THE SOUTH RIM

BY CAR

Exploring the South Rim in your own car lets you hop from sight to sight at your own pace, but traffic and parking can be a pain during the busy summer months. And from March 1 through November 30, Hermit Road and the road to Yaki Point are closed to private vehicle traffic. Often it's best to park your car at one of the five parking areas in Grand Canyon Village (p.122) and use the park's free shuttle system. You'll need a car, however, to explore Desert View Drive, which is not serviced by the shuttles.

BY SHUTTLE

The park runs free shuttle buses that make frequent stops in Grand Canyon Village and along Hermit Drive. Exact schedules vary from season to season, so pick up a copy of the park's free newspaper, *The Guide*, for current schedules and other information. The most popular shuttle routes are the **Village Route**, which loops through parking areas, viewpoints and lodges in Grand Canyon Village, and the **Hermits Rest Route**, which runs back and forth along Hermit Drive. Two additional shuttles provide access to the South Kaibab Trail trailhead at Yaki Point; the **Kaibab Trail Route** runs between the Canyon View Information Plaza and Yaki Point, and the **Hiker's Express Route** shuttles early morning hikers from Bright Angel Lodge and the Backcountry Information Center to Yaki Point.

ON FOOT

One of the best ways to explore the South Rim is to walk along the **Rim Trail**, which stretches from Pipe Creek Vista, about a half mile south of Mather Point (p.124), to Hermits Rest (p.154). From end to end the Rim Trail is 13 miles long, but you can pick it up at any point. Even better, park shuttles service just about every sight between Mather Point and Hermits Rest, which allows you to hike to a distant point, then ride a shuttle back.

BY BICYCLE

Bicycles are allowed on all paved and unpaved roads on the South Rim, but they're prohibited from all other trails (including the Rim Trail). If passing cars don't bother you, bicycles are one of the best ways to explore the South Rim. But keep in mind that bicyclists must obey all traffic regulations. And when riding on narrow Hermit Road, bicyclists should pull to the right shoulder of the road and dismount when large vehicles are attempting to pass.

DINING

All restaurants on the South Rim are located in Grand Canyon Village (with the sole exception of a small cafeteria at Desert View). During the busy summer months, restaurants that don't accept reservations fill up fast and wait times can sometimes exceed two hours. If you want to beat the crowds, arrive before sunset.

ARIZONA ROOM

This popular dinner spot, located in Bright Angel Lodge, serves standard American food. Open 4:30 p.m.–10 p.m. No reservations.

BRIGHT ANGEL RESTAURANT

Serves breakfast, lunch and dinner in Bright Angel Lodge. Open 6:30 a.m.–10 p.m. No reservations.

EL TOVAR

The finest (and most expensive) dining in the park. Prices top $20 an entree, with no extra charge for the soft lighting and dark wood paneling. Reservations, often made days in advance, are only available for dinner. Open for breakfast, lunch and dinner (928-638-2526 x6432).

MASWIK CAFETERIA

Cafeteria-style fast food with Mexican and Italian selections. Open 6 a.m.–10 p.m.

YAVAPAI CAFETERIA

Cafeteria-style fast food. Open 7 a.m.–8 p.m. (6 a.m.–9 p.m. in the summer).

ENTERTAINMENT

RANGER PROGRAMS

Free ranger programs are offered throughout the year. Topics include history, geology, wildlife and more. Highly recommended. Check *The Guide* for exact times and locations.

BUS TOURS

Xanterra (the same company that runs the park's lodges) offers narrated bus tours along the South Rim. The **Desert View Tour** (4 hours, $30) travels along Desert View Drive. The **Hermit Road Tour** (2 hours, $15) travels along Hermit Drive. Sunrise and sunset tours ($12) also run May–October, and a package deal offering two tours is available for $35. Children under 16 ride for free. For more info contact the transportation desk at any lodge.

MULE TRIPS

Day and overnight mule trips depart daily from the South Rim. **Day trips** (7 hours, \$130 per person) descend 3,500 feet down the Bright Angel Trail (p.170) to Plateau Point (p.176), then return via the same route. **Overnight trips** follow the Bright Angel Trail to the bottom, where riders spend the night at Phantom Ranch (p.115), then return the next day via the South Kaibab Trail (p.178); Cost: \$350 for one person, \$625 for two people. Rides offering an extra night at Phantom Ranch are also available November–March. Reservations should be made as far in advance as possible (they're accepted up to one year in advance). Contact Xanterra for additional info (888-297-2757, www.grandcanyonlodges.com).

ART EXHIBITS

Kolb Studio (p.140) showcases constantly changing art exhibits. Check *The Guide* for info on the current exhibit.

GRAND CANYON MUSIC FESTIVAL

Weekend and mid-week concerts are offered every September at the Shrine of the Ages. Tickets: \$25 adults, \$8 children (www.grandcanyonmusicfest.org).

SERVICES

CANYON VILLLAGE MARKETPLACE

This general store in Market Plaza (next to Yavapai Lodge) sells groceries, film, camping gear, outdoor supplies and a wide selection of other items. Open 8 a.m.–7 p.m. (7 a.m.–8:30 p.m. in the summer).

GAS

There are no gas stations in Grand Canyon Village. The closest gas stations are in the town of Tusayan and at Desert View.

POST OFFICE

Located in Market Plaza. Open every weekday and half-day Saturday.

COIN-OPERATED SHOWERS & LAUNDROMAT

Located near the entrance to Mather Campground.

PET KENNEL

Offers lodging for pets (which aren't allowed in park lodges or on inner canyon trails). Reservations are recommended (928-638-0534).

GRAND CANYON GARAGE

Offers auto repair, emergency 24-hour service, and towing (928-638-2631).

Tusayan BASICS

Tusayan is a small town located a few miles south of Grand Canyon Village. Built entirely around Grand Canyon tourism, the town consists of a short stretch of hotels, restaurants and shops along AZ-64. Just south of the shops is tiny Grand Canyon Airport, which offers sightseeing flights (p.31).

LODGING

Lodging in Tusayan is (surprisingly) often more expensive than lodging in the park. The reason: many of Tusayan's hotels offer modern luxuries such as swimming pools and spas that are unavailable in the park. Room rates listed below are for peak tourist season (winter rates are generally lower).

BEST WESTERN GRAND CANYON SQUIRE INN

One of the most extravagant options in Tusayan. Offers large rooms, an outdoor pool, tennis courts, spa, sports bar, three restaurants, and a bowling alley (800-622-6966, www.grandcanyonsquire.com).
Rates: $150–$225

GRAND CANYON QUALITY INN

Standard chain motel with an outdoor pool and indoor hot tub (800-221-2222, www.grandcanyonqualityinn.com).
Rates: $160–$210

THE GRAND HOTEL

A modern hotel with a classic lodge design. Offers an indoor pool, restaurant and live entertainment (888-634-7263, www.visitgrandcanyon.com).
Rates: $160–$190

HOLIDAY INN EXPRESS

Standard chain motel with an indoor pool and spa. Also offers Kids Suites with bunk beds, TV, VCR and video games (888-473-2269, www.gcanyon.com/hi).
Rates: $150–$160

RODEWAY INN RED FEATHER LODGE

Budget motel with outdoor pool, hot tub, and fitness center (800-538-2345, www.redfeatherlodge.com). **Rates:** $100–$160

CAMPING

GRAND CANYON CAMPER VILLAGE

Offers tent sites ($25) and RV sites ($50, full hook-up). Coin-operated showers nearby. Reservations only available for RV sites with hook-ups (928-638-2887).

TEN X CAMPGROUND

Operated by the Kaibab National Forest, two miles south of Tusayan. Open May–September, Cost: $10 per vehicle (928-638-2443).

DINING

CAFE TUSAYAN

Standard American food. Located next to the Red Feather Lodge.

CANYON STAR

American and southwestern food. Located in the Grand Hotel (928-638-3333).

CORONADO ROOM

American and southwestern food. Open only for dinner. Located in the Best Western Grand Canyon Squire (928-638-2681).

YIPPEI-EI-O! STEAKHOUSE

Classic steakhouse. Open for lunch (summer only) and dinner (928-638-2780).

WE COOK PIZZA AND PASTA

Serves, you guessed it, pizza and pasta. Open for lunch and dinner (928-638-2278).

ENTERTAINMENT

IMAX THEATER

Year after year, the IMAX film *Grand Canyon—The Hidden Secrets* lures hordes of visitors to this 70-foot screen. Although the story is hardly Oscar-caliber, the scenery is undeniably breathtaking. The 35-minute movie plays every hour on the half hour. Cost: $10 adults, $7 children under 12.

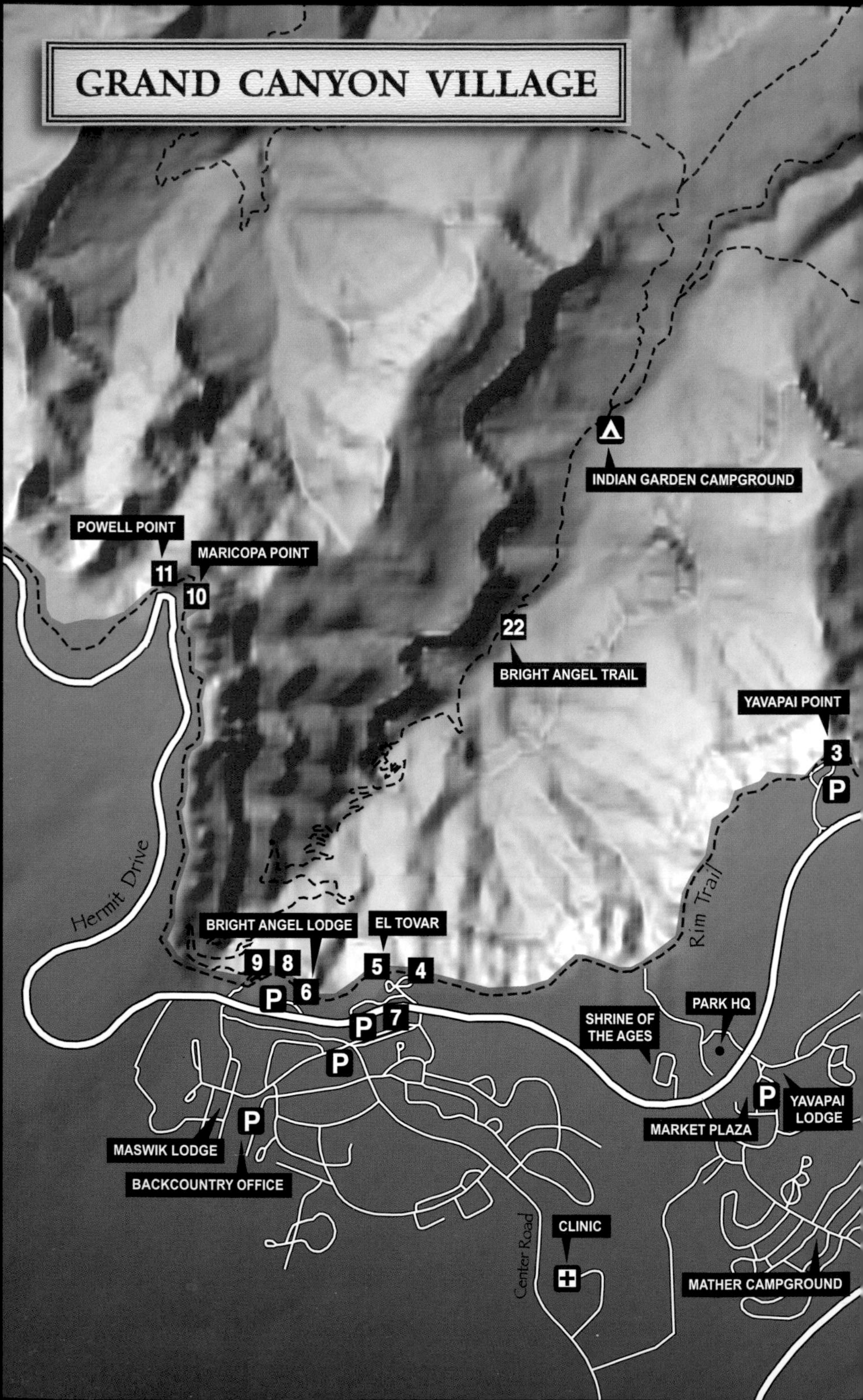

GRAND CANYON VILLAGE
INDIAN GARDEN CAMPGROUND
POWELL POINT
11
MARICOPA POINT
10
22
BRIGHT ANGEL TRAIL
YAVAPAI POINT
3
P
Hermit Drive
Rim Trail
BRIGHT ANGEL LODGE
EL TOVAR
9
8
5
4
P
6
P
7
P
PARK HQ
SHRINE OF THE AGES
P
YAVAPAI LODGE
MARKET PLAZA
P
MASWIK LODGE
BACKCOUNTRY OFFICE
CLINIC
Center Road
MATHER CAMPGROUND

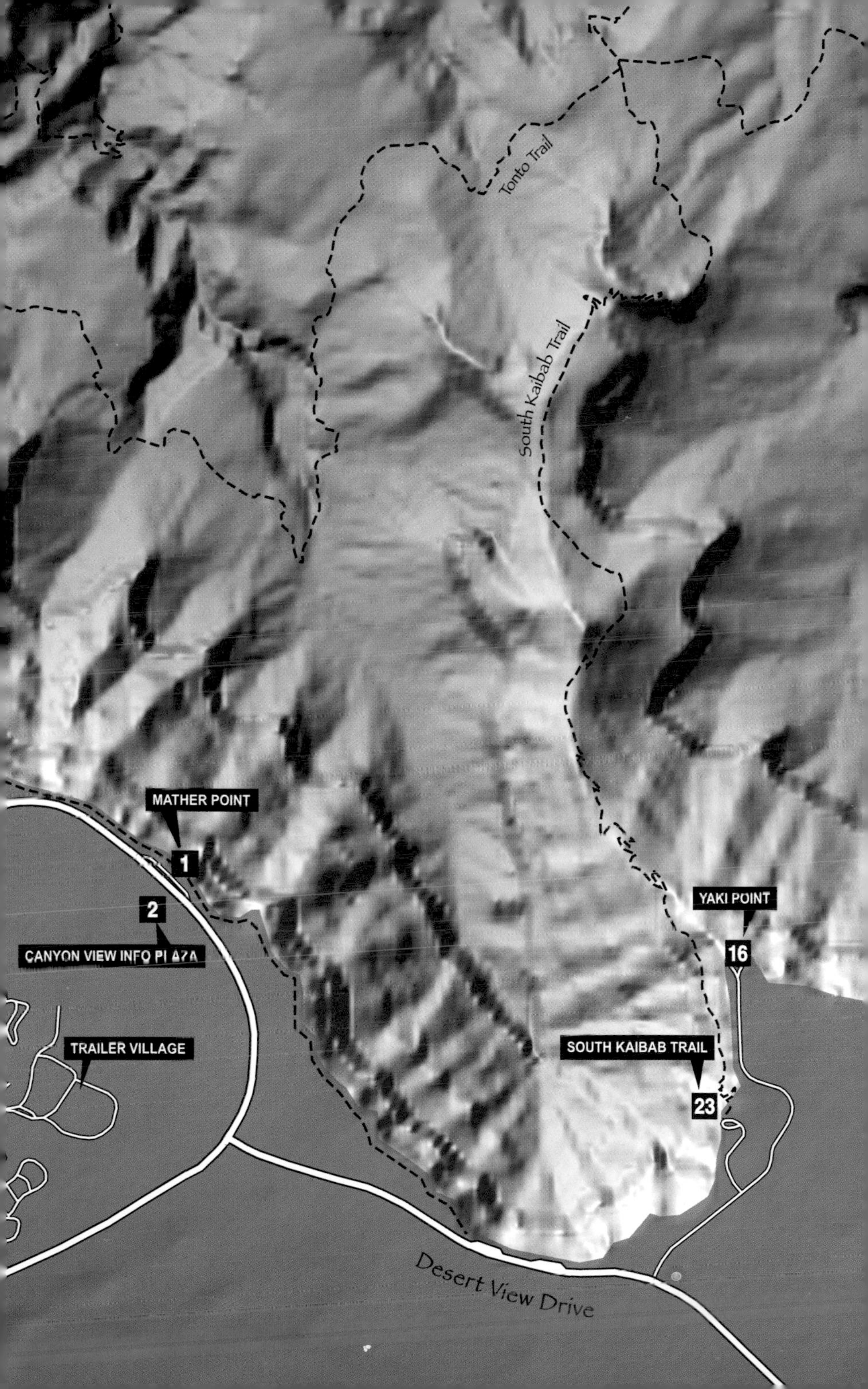
Tonto Trail
South Kaibab Trail
MATHER POINT
1
2
CANYON VIEW INFO PLAZA
TRAILER VILLAGE
YAKI POINT
16
SOUTH KAIBAB TRAIL
23
Desert View Drive

1 Mather Point

Mather Point is the most popular viewpoint in the park, but that's mostly because of it's close proximity to the park entrance. Regardless, the views are fantastic. Although the scenery stretches on for miles, only about one third of the total length of the Grand Canyon is visible. Among the famous landmarks visible from Mather Point: O'Neill Butte (above) and Vishnu Temple (left). Vishnu Temple rises to a height of 7,533 feet and was named by the early geologist Clarence Dutton, who felt it bore "a surprising resemblance to an Oriental pagoda."

Mather Point is named for Stephen Mather, the first director of the National Park Service. In 1914 Mather, then a retired millionaire, complained to Interior Secretary Franklin Lane about the management of America's national parks. Lane's response: "If you don't like the way the national parks are being run, come on down to Washington and run them yourself." Mather did just that. He joined the National Park Service in 1916 and spent the next 13 years of his life shaping a strong vision for America's national parks.

Although the views from Mather Point are stunning, its popularity makes it one of the most congested spots in the park, *especially* in the summer. Savvy visitors realize there are equally fantastic viewpoints nearby, such as Yaki Point (p.158) to the east and as Yavapai Point (p.129) to the west. If the crowds at Mather Point are overwhelming, don't hesitate to move on. You can always come back later.

Note: Parking is limited to 60 minutes at Mather Point.

Vishnu Temple

2 Canyon View Info Plaza

This complex of buildings, nestled in the woods across from Mather Point, serves as the park's main welcoming center. On the right is the visitor center, which features a ranger-staffed help desk and several exhibits about the park. Across the way is Books & More, a store operated by the non-profit Grand Canyon Association that sells books, maps, postcards and more. Restrooms are located nearby.

Canyon View Information Plaza, which opened in 2000, was originally intended as the terminus of a light rail system that would shuttle visitors into the park from large parking lots in Tusayan. Visitors could leave their cars in Tusayan, hop the train to Canyon View Information Plaza, and then explore the South Rim using the park's free shuttle system. (The open air exhibits were built to give visitors something to look at while they waited for the train.) Unfortunately, budgetary issues have delayed construction of the light rail.

Canyon View Information Plaza is open 8 a.m.–6 p.m. May–mid-October, 8 a.m.–5 p.m. the rest of the year.

Note: There's no parking at Canyon View Information Plaza. The closest parking is at Mather Point. If the parking area at Mather Point is full, you can park in Grand Canyon Village and hop a free shuttle back to Canyon View Information Plaza or follow the new Greenway Trail, a walking and biking trail that links Grand Canyon Village with Canyon View Information Plaza.

GRAND CANYON
A Spectacular Part of the Colorado Plateau

Bright Angel Canyon

3 Yavapai Point

Yavapai Observation Center, perched right on the edge of Yavapai Point, is a historic building that served as the South Rim's first museum and interpretive center. Originally built in 1928, it has large viewing windows that provide sweeping panoramas of the Canyon, making it a great place to take shelter in bad weather. Inside there are exhibits and a small store selling books and postcards. Restrooms are located in a building next to the parking area.

One of the most prominent sights from Yavapai Point is Bright Angel Canyon, which slices eight miles into the North Rim. The North Kaibab Trail (p.280) runs through much of Bright Angel Canyon. As the trail nears the Colorado River it passes by Phantom Ranch, a collection of small buildings offering the only overnight lodging at the bottom of Grand Canyon. Phantom Ranch is visible from Yavapai Point; look for the faint patch of green foliage running east-west at the head of Bright Angel Canyon.

Another famous feature visible from Yavapai Point is the broad, flat Tonto Platform, located just above the dark Inner Gorge near the bottom of the Canyon. Eagle-eyed visitors can spot the faint Tonto Trail running east-west along the Tonto Platform south of the Colorado River.

Yavapai is a Paiute Indian word that means "Sun People." The word refers to a group of Indians who once lived in central and western Arizona.

4 Hopi House

Hopi House was designed by Mary Colter, a famous architect who designed many of the park's historic buildings. Patterned after buildings at Old Orabai (a Hopi Village 80 miles east of Grand Canyon that is the oldest continuously inhabited town in America), Hopi House was Colter's first assignment for the park. Hopi Indians helped in its construction, and the stone exterior, corner fireplaces, and thatched ceilings are all characteristic of Hopi design. After the building opened in 1905 Hopi craftsmen lived on its upper floors for many years. Nightly Hopi dances were also common during this time. Today crafts from several Southwestern tribes are sold inside.

MARY COLTER

During the early 1900s, a time when few women practiced architecture, Mary Colter was hard at work designing some of the most spectacular buildings in the Southwest, many of which are now listed as historic landmarks. Among her Grand Canyon creations: Lookout Studio, Hermits Rest, Desert View Watchtower, and Phantom Ranch.

5 El Tovar Hotel

El Tovar is the finest in Grand Canyon. The historic building, designed by architect Charles Whittlesey, was one of the most elegant and technologically advanced hotels in the Southwest when it opened in 1905. Among its high-tech amenities: electric lights, steam heat, hot and cold water, and indoor plumbing—a stark contrast to the primitive rooms, cheap beds and outhouses that had previously defined opulence at Grand Canyon. When El Tovar first opened, its 100 rooms *doubled* the total number of hotel rooms on the South Rim. For many years fresh fruits and vegetables were grown in El Tovar's greenhouses, and local farm animals provided fresh eggs and milk.

El Tovar was named after Don Pedro de Tovar, a lieutenant of Spanish explorer Francisco Vasquez de Coronado, who led the first Spanish expedition through the Southwest in 1540. Ironically, Don Pedro de Tovar never set eyes on Grand Canyon. But the Fred Harvey Company, the builders of the hotel, already had a Cardenas Hotel in Colorado, so the name El Tovar was chosen instead.

Over the years El Tovar has played host to such 20th century icons as Theodore Roosevelt, Albert Einstein, and Paul McCartney. Today the hotel continues to offer the finest lodging and dining in the park. Even if you're not a guest, El Tovar is worth at least a quick look in the front lobby, or a long drink at the hotel bar.

6 Bright Angel Lodge

Bright Angel Lodge offers some of the best budget lodging in Grand Canyon, with a stunning location right on the rim. When it first opened in 1896, the lodge consisted of nothing more than a collection of primitive tents. Guests walked from tent to tent along an elevated boardwalk that protected them from horse droppings (a prominent feature of Grand Canyon Village back then). Over the years, the lodge expanded to include a log cabin with eight guest rooms. Cabin rooms were rented for $2.50 per night, and tents were rented for $1.50. The lodge later expanded, and the current buildings were built in the 1930s.

Inside Bright Angel Lodge you'll find a restaurant, a bar, and a gift shop. There's also a small museum with a fireplace built out of actual Grand Canyon rocks—arranged floor to ceiling in their proper geological sequence. A small booth to the left of the front desk offers information on ranger programs, bus tours, mule rides, and other daily activities.

Note: Bright Angel Lodge is the closest lodge to the Bright Angel Trail, something well worth considering if you're planning a grueling hike on the trail.

View near Bright Angel Lodge

7 Santa Fe Train Depot

This train station, located just south of El Tovar Hotel, is the only train station in any U.S. national park and (supposedly) the last surviving train station in America built entirely out of logs.

Train service first arrived at the South Rim in 1901, following the completion of a spur line connecting the South Rim to the town of Williams, 60 miles to the south. Before the spur line was completed, the most dependable form of transportation to the South Rim was a bumpy, all-day stagecoach ride that coast $20. When the spur line was completed, visitors could travel to the rim in about four hours for $3.50. Not surprisingly, the railroad brought a flood of new visitors to the South Rim. But several decades later most people were arriving by car, and in 1968 falling ridership forced the railroad to shut down. (The last departing train carried only three passengers.) Then, in 1989, the railroad roared back to life. With traffic and congestion increasing in the park, a new generation of riders rediscovered the railroad's convenience and charm. Today, trains depart daily from Williams.

8 Lookout Studio

This small rough-hewn building, located just west of Bright Angel Lodge, is perched right on the edge of the Canyon. It offers stunning views of the Canyon and a small gift shop inside. Lookout Studio was designed by Mary Colter, whose wanted it to blend seamlessly into the landscape, creating as little visual disturbance with the scenery as possible. This followed the design principles set forth by renowned landscape architect Fredrick Law Olmstead, who believed that, whenever possible, buildings in national parks should reflect the architecture of indigenous cultures. The indigenous cultures of the Southwest built some of the most impressive structures in ancient America, and Colter incorporated many of their architectural techniques such as stone walls, flat roofs, and timber supports into her design.

Lookout Studio has long been famous for its views. An old Santa Fe Railroad brochure once boasted that visitors who peered through the telescopes installed at Lookout Studio could, "traverse the Canyon trails, explore the rugged portions of the interior, or see its faraway reaches."

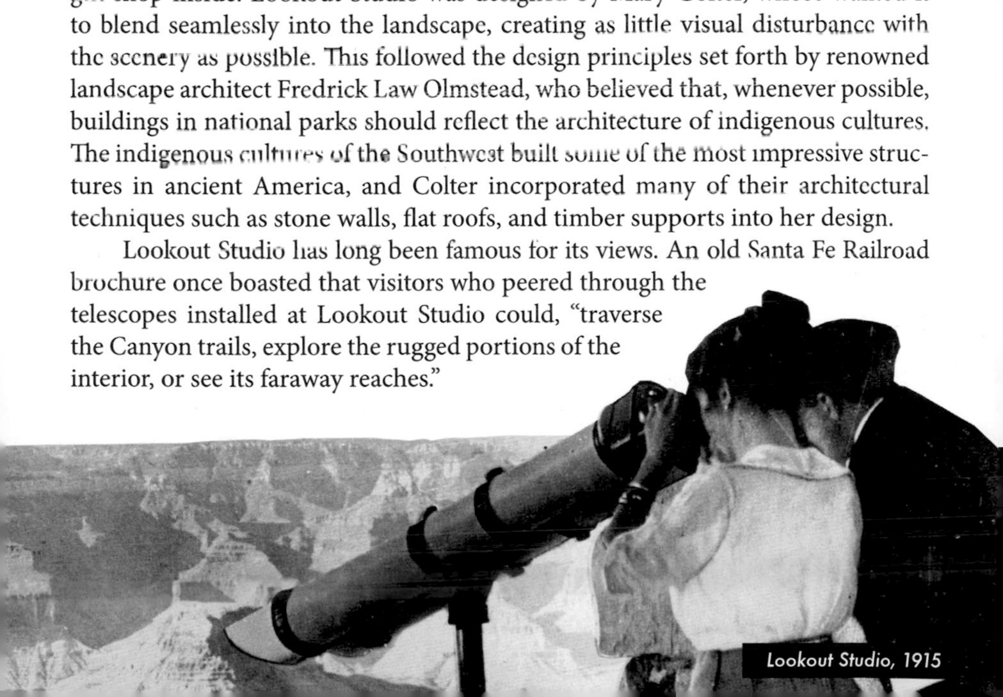

Lookout Studio, 1915

9 Kolb Studio

Today Kolb Studio houses a well-stocked bookstore and art gallery with changing exhibits. But for over 70 years it was the home of Emery Kolb, one of Grand Canyon's earliest and most famous photographers. Emery came to Grand Canyon with his brother, Ellsworth, in 1902. Shortly after their arrival, the brothers set up a photography studio on the rim and started hawking souvenir photos of mule riders descending the nearby Bright Angel Trail. But as Saturday Evening Post writer Irvin S. Cobb wrote of one such mule ride, "Just under the first terrace a halt is made while the official photographer takes a picture; and when you get back he has your finished copy ready for you, so you can see for yourself just how pale and haggard and wall-eyed and how much like a typhoid patient you looked."

Tourist photos paid the bills, but the Kolb brothers' true passion was exploring Grand Canyon and capturing their daredevil exploits on film. In 1911 the brothers ran the Colorado River from Wyoming to California—the first time anyone had accomplished the feat since John Wesley Powell's historic journey in 1869. But the Kolbs' trip wasn't simply for the record books. The brothers filmed their journey to make the first-ever movie of a river trip through Grand Canyon. The Kolbs screened their movie at lectures across the country, and it played continuously at Kolb Studio until Emery's death in 1976.

Emery Kolb

The Kolb brothers

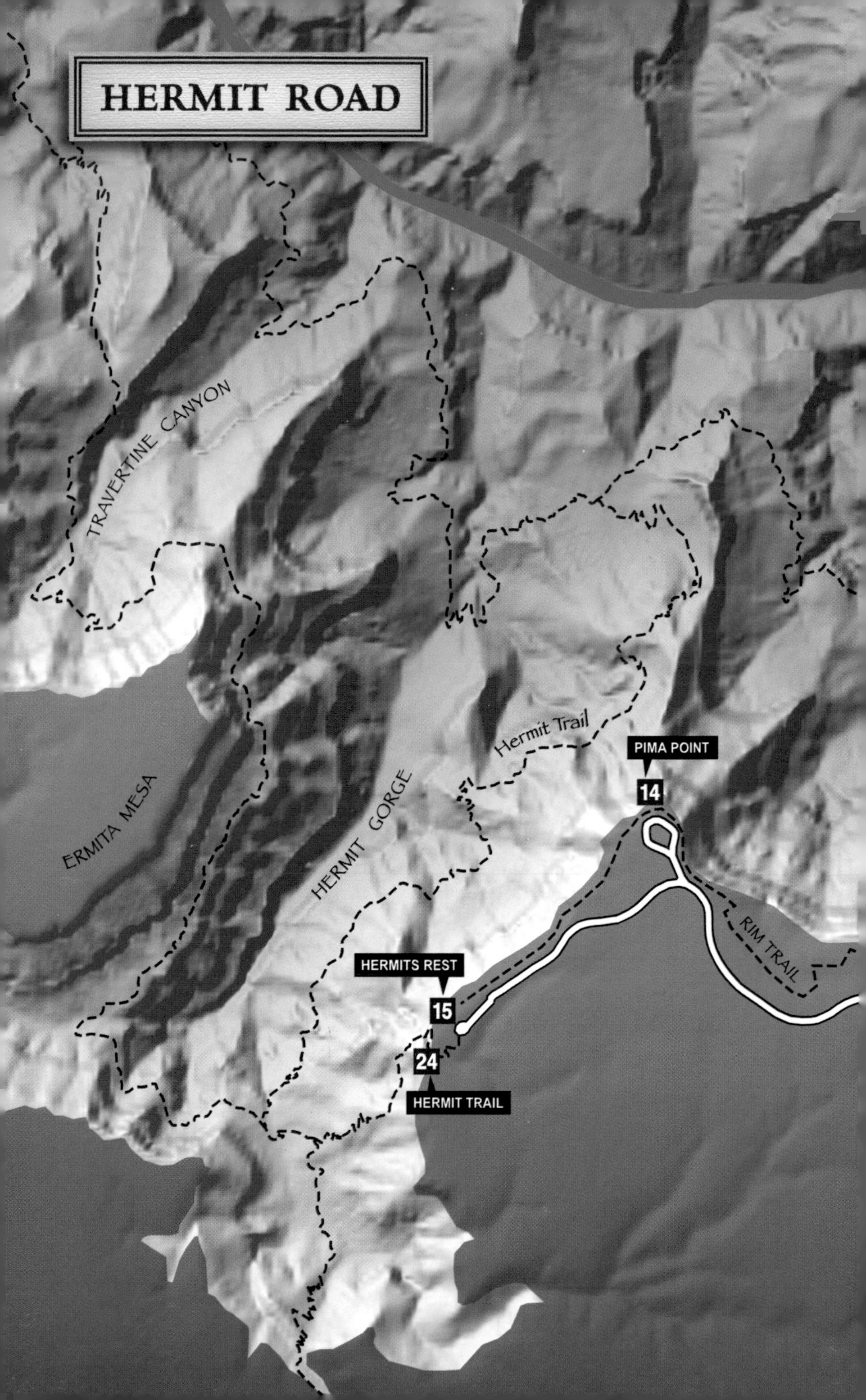
HERMIT ROAD
TRAVERTINE CANYON
ERMITA MESA
HERMIT GORGE
Hermit Trail
PIMA POINT
14
RIM TRAIL
HERMITS REST
15
24
HERMIT TRAIL

Tonto Trail
THE ALLIGATOR
THE BATTLESHIP
HOPI POINT
MOHAVE POINT
POWELL POINT
MARICOPA POINT
13
12
11
10
Bright Angel Trail
BRIGHT ANGEL LODGE
EL TOVAR
9
8
6
5
4
P
7
THE ABYSS
The South Rim

10 Maricopa Point

Maricopa Point offers Hermit Road's first sweeping views of western Grand Canyon. Just west of the point is a large metal frame that marks the remains of the Lost Orphan Mine, one of the most production uranium mines in America in the 1950s. Several decades earlier, a privately owned resort was located on the same spot. It consisted of 20 cabins, a trading post, and a saloon. At one point the resort was owned by Will Rogers, Jr., who named it "Roger's Place."

"Imagine, if you can, a monster of a hollow approximately some hundreds of miles long and a mile deep, and anywhere from ten to sixteen miles wide, with a mountain range—the most wonderful mountain range in the world—planted in it . . . Imagine all this spread out beneath the unflawed turquoise of the Arizona sky and washed in the liquid gold of the Arizona sunshine—and if you imagine hard enough and keep it up long enough you may begin, in the course of eight or ten years, to have a faint, a very faint and shadowy conception of this spot where the shamed scheme of creation is turned upside down and the very womb of the world is laid bare before our imperious eyes. Then go to Arizona and see it all for yourself, and you will realize what an entirely inadequate and deficient thing the human imagination is."

—Irvin S. Cobb, Roughing It, Deluxe, 1913

11 Powell Point

Powell Point is named for John Wesley Powell, the famous explorer who led the first Colorado River expedition through Grand Canyon in 1869. In 1920 a monument to Powell was built and dedicated here. The ceremony was attended by Powell's niece and grand-niece, and the monument was christened by the Secretary of the Interior with water from the Colorado River.

Powell's Grand Canyon adventure has often been called the last great expedition of the American West. Prior to the trip, no one knew what existed along much of the Colorado River. There were rumors of giant waterfalls at the bottom of Grand Canyon and places where the river disappeared underground. Accepting these risks, Powell, a one-armed Civil War veteran, and nine other men (none with any whitewater experience) launched four boats from Green River, Wyoming in May 1869. Three months later, two boats carrying six skeletal men emerged from Grand Canyon near present-day Lake Mead. Four men had abandoned the grueling journey along the way, three of whom died trying to reach civilization. The names of those four men do not appear on the monument. See page 81 for more on Powell's extraordinary journey.

12 Hopi Point

Hopi Point offers some of Hermit Road's most sweeping views of the Canyon. It was named in honor of the Hopi Indians.

Several famous geologic features are visible from Hopi Point, including Shiva Temple (named for the Hindu destroyer), Isis Temple (named for the Egyptian goddess of nature), and Cheops Pyramid (named for the Great Pyramid of Cheops). Shiva Temple was named by 19th-century geologist Clarence Dutton, who wrote, "In such a stupendous scene of wreck it seems as if the fabled 'Destroyer' might find an abode not wholly uncongenial." Shiva Temple is one of the largest buttes in the Canyon, rising 4,000 feet from its base with a 300-acre flat top. This "sky island" has probably been separated from the North Rim for over 100,000 years. Today, thrill-seeking rock-climbers test their mettle on its sheer walls.

"At length, as the sun draws near the horizon, the great drama of the day begins . . . Slowly the myriad of details have come out and the walls are flecked with lines of minute tracery . . . Stronger and sharper becomes the relief of each projection . . . The colossal buttes expand in every dimension. Their long, narrow wings, which once were folded together and flattened against each other, open out, disclosing between them vast alcoves illuminated with Rembrandt lights . . . A thousand forms, hitherto unseen or obscure, start up within the abyss, and stand forth in strength and animation. All things seem to grow in beauty, power, and dimensions. What was grand before has become majestic, the majestic becomes sublime, and, ever expanding and developing, the sublime passes beyond the reach of our faculties and becomes transcendent."

—Clarence Dutton, A Tertiary History of the Grand Canyon District, 1882

13 Mohave Point

Mohave Point is named in honor of the Mojave Indians, who once lived along the lower Colorado River south of Grand Canyon. And no, that's not a typo you just saw. As a general rule, Mojave is spelled with a "j" when referring to place names in California, and with an "h" when referring to place names in Arizona.

The long, rocky promontory that stretches down from Mohave Point is called the Alligator. It was named by long-time Canyon resident Emery Kolb, who thought the low ridge looked like the back of an alligator. Hermit Rapid, on the Colorado River, is also visible from Mohave Point. The rapid, like many in Grand Canyon, formed when debris washed into the river from an adjacent side canyon. It's possible to hike to Hermit Rapid along the popular Hermit Trail (p.184).

"Imagine, way down there at the bottom, a stream visible only at certain favored points because of the mighty intervening ribs and chines of rock—a stream that appears to you as a torpidly crawling yellow worm, its wrinkling back spangled with tarnished white specks, but which is really a wide, deep, brawling, rushing river—the Colorado—full of torrents and rapids; and those white specks you see are the tops of enormous rocks in its bed."

—Irvin S. Cobb, Roughing It, Deluxe, 1913

Hermit Rapid

14 Pima Point

Pima Point, named after the Pima Indians of southern Arizona, offers one of the best views of the Colorado River along the South Rim. Although the Pima Indians refer to themselves as *Akimel O'odham* ("River People"), the name Pima is derived from *pim'ach*, which means "I don't understand you." This was probably the unfortunate response given to early Spanish explorers when they asked the *Akimel O'odham* what they called themselves.

In 1912 the Fred Harvey Company built an upscale cluster of tent cabins 3,600 feet below Pima Point. This retreat, called Hermit Camp, was located along the Hermit Trail, the Santa Fe Railroad's free alternative to the Bright Angel Trail, which was then operated as a private toll road (p.96). The camp boasted such amenities as showers, telephones, a dining hall, a stable, and a blacksmith's shop. Guests generally stayed for several days, spending their time exploring the rugged surroundings on foot or horseback.

In 1926 a 6,300-foot aerial tram was built connecting Pima Point and Hermit Camp. At the time it was the longest single-span tram in the United States. The tram ride was about a half hour each way, but this modern marvel did not last long. In the late 1920s the park service gained control of the Bright Angel Trail, which was located closer to popular hotels on the rim, and lifted its toll. Before long, most Grand Canyon visitors were descending the Canyon via the Bright Angel Trail and spending the night at Phantom Ranch. In 1930 Hermit Camp shut down for good. Its remains were burned and the tram was removed.

Hermit Camp

15 Hermits Rest

Hermits Rest marks the end of Hermit Road. Its main attraction is a whimsical stone building with a gift shop inside. Drinks, snacks and restrooms are also available.

Hermits Rest was built by the Santa Fe Railroad in 1914. Like many famous buildings in the park, it was designed by architect Mary Colter, whose wanted to create a building that looked as if a hermit might live there. In addition to the main building, famous for its large fireplace, she also designed a limestone arch with an authentic New Mexico mission bell.

Hermits Rest was inspired by an early prospector named Louis Boucher, who lived by himself in the canyon below. Although labeled a hermit, Boucher was, by all accounts, a friendly man who simply preferred living alone. Originally from Quebec, Boucher arrived at Grand Canyon around 1891. He kept a variety of animals including horses, mules and goldfish (which he kept in a trough). Boucher also planted an orchard that provided him with peaches, oranges and figs. After spending two decades searching in vain for a rich mineral strike, Boucher moved to Utah in 1909.

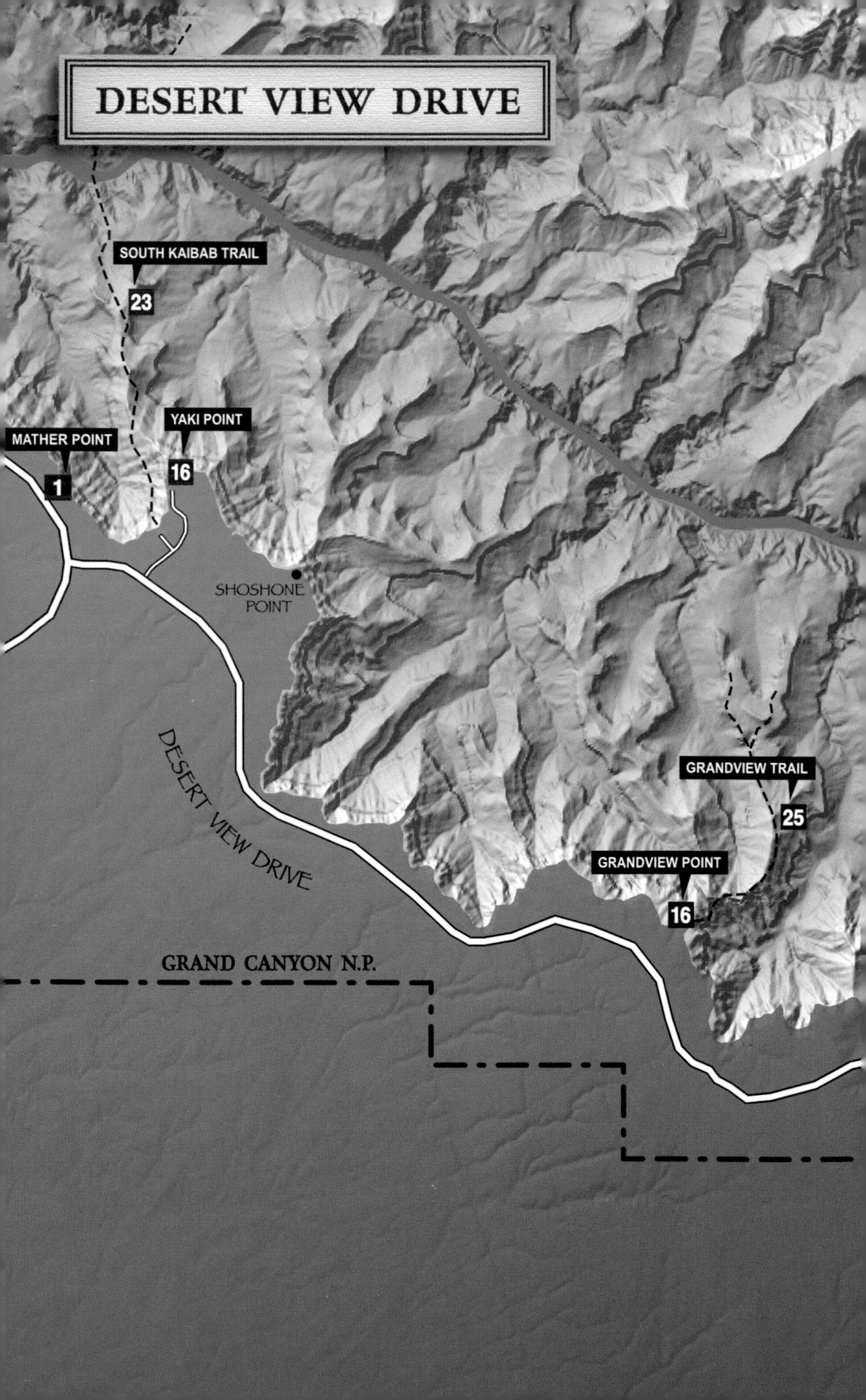
DESERT VIEW DRIVE
SOUTH KAIBAB TRAIL
23
MATHER POINT
1
YAKI POINT
16
SHOSHONE POINT
DESERT VIEW DRIVE
GRANDVIEW TRAIL
25
GRANDVIEW POINT
16
GRAND CANYON N.P.

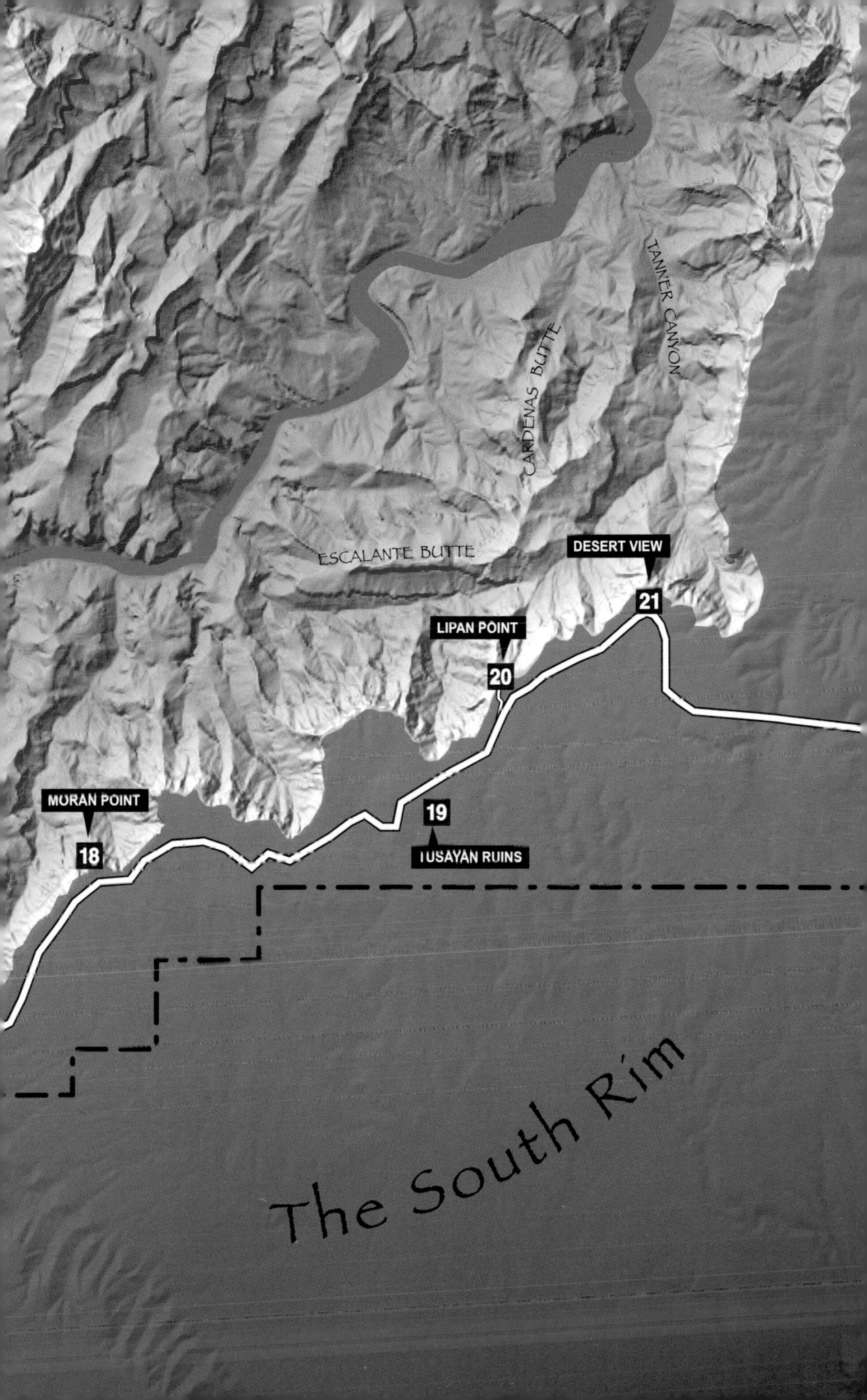

TANNER CANYON
CARDENAS BUTTE
ESCALANTE BUTTE
DESERT VIEW
21
LIPAN POINT
20
MORAN POINT
18
19
TUSAYAN RUINS
The South Rim

16 Yaki Point

Stretching far into the Canyon, Yaki Point provides sweeping views to the east and west, making it one of the best sunrise spots on the South Rim. Yaki Point was supposedly named by George Wharton James in honor of Mexico's Yaqui Indians, who were victims of mass genocide in the early 1900s.

The South Kaibab Trail, which offers the South Rim's most direct route to the bottom of the Canyon, starts just south of Yaki Point (p.180). It is one of the few trails in the park that does not follow a historic Indian path.

Note: Unless you visit in the winter, the road to Yaki Point is closed to private vehicle traffic. It can be reached via the park's free shuttle (p.117).

"Imagine—if it be winter—snowdrifts above, with desert flowers blooming alongside the drifts, and down below great stretches of green verdure; imagine two or three separate snowstorms visibly raging at different points, with clear, bright stretches of distance intervening between them, and nearer maybe a splendid rainbow arching downward into the great void; for these meteorological three-ring circuses are not uncommon at certain seasons."

—Irvin S. Cobb, Roughing It, Deluxe, 1913

17 Grandview Point

At 7,406 feet, Grandview Point is one of the highest points on the South Rim. In addition to its views—which are indeed grand—Grandview Point is notable for its concentration of ponderosa pines, which grow only at high elevations. Grandview Point is also the jumping off point for the popular Grandview Trail (p.190).

Before the railroad arrived at Grand Canyon Village in 1901, Grandview Point was the hub of all tourist activity in the park. In 1886 John Hance, a prospector turned tour guide (p.90), built the first hotel here. Within a few years another prospector named Pete Berry had built the Grandview Hotel (above) nearby. But when the railroad arrived in Grand Canyon Village a decade later, few tourists were willing to make the additional trek to Grandview Point, and by 1908 both hotels had shut down. A few years later, Berry sold his landholdings to newspaper tycoon William Randolf Hearst, who tore down the Grandview Hotel in 1929. Hearst planned to build his own hotel on the property, but a federal court forced him to sell his land to the park in 1939.

During its short-lived hotel era, Grandview Point was a popular jumping off point for miners seeking mineral riches below the rim. In 1890 Pete Berry, Ralph Cameron (p.96), and Niles Cameron established the Last Chance copper mine at Horseshoe Mesa, just below Grandview Point. The mine contained an extremely high-grade ore (up to 70 percent copper), but when copper prices crashed in 1907 mining operations at Last Chance shut down.

18 Moran Point

This pleasant overlook is named after Thomas Moran, one of America's most famous and influential landscape painters. Although born in England in 1837, Moran moved to America with his family in the mid-1800s, a time when American landscape painting exhibitions were drawing blockbuster crowds in large cities. In the days before photography, landscape painting allowed people to view some of America's most remote, beautiful places. Inspired by these works, Moran decided to become a landscape painter himself. His dramatic paintings of Yellowstone were critical in the establishment of Yellowstone National Park in 1872. The following year, Moran joined legendary explorer John Wesley Powell on an expedition to Grand Canyon. He later wrote of his experience, "it was by far the most awfully grand and impressive scene that I have ever yet seen." Moran later returned with geologist Clarence Dutton, and his works from both of these trips were later published in best-selling books. One of his paintings, "The Grand Chasm of the Colorado," hung in the U.S. Capitol for many years. Deeply moved by his Grand Canyon experiences, Moran returned to the canyon every winter between 1899 and 1920.

Thomas Moran, with daughters

Large Kiva

19 Tusayan Ruin

These ruins mark the location of Tusayan, a small Ancestral Puebloan village that existed here 800 years ago. The remains were partially excavated in 1930, and today they are the most visited archaeological site in Arizona (a distinction that has more to do with its high-traffic Grand Canyon location than the ruins themselves, which are somewhat underwhelming). A 0.1-mile path guides visitors through the ruins, and free ranger tours are offered that help bring Tusayan to life. A small museum is also located near the parking area.

At its peak, Tusayan was probably home to no more than 30 people, and archaeologists believe that it was only occupied for about 20 years. Tusayan one of the last Ancestral Puebloan sites occupied in Grand Canyon, constructed shortly before the collapse of Ancestral Puebloan society around A.D. 1200. The most prominent feature of the village was a large, 14-room building with two kivas (ceremonial rooms) located nearby. Crops such as beans, corn and squash were grown in a field to the east, but because there is no permanent source of water within seven miles of Tusayan, stone walls were built in the fields to retain runoff. Despite this access to fresh food, evidence indicates that health problems were common among Ancestral Puebloans. Chimney's and windows were largely absent from their structures, and smoke-filled rooms contributed to respiratory difficulties. Skeletal remains also reveal teeth worn down to the dentine, the result of eating stone-ground cornmeal.

20 Lipan Point

Lipan Point offers one of the most sweeping views on the South Rim. It's also one of the best places to see rocks of the Grand Canyon Supergroup, which range in age from 800 million to 1.2 billion years old. Although rocks of the Grand Canyon Supergroup are absent from much of the canyon, they are easy to identify because they have been tilted at a roughly 20-degree angle (above).

Cardenas Butte, which lies just east of Escalente Butte (right), was named in honor of Garcias Lopez de Cardenas, who led a group of Spanish explorers to a spot near Lipan Point in 1540 (p.77).

"Imagine these mountain peaks—hundreds upon hundreds of them—rising one behind the other, stretching away in endless, serried rank until the eye swims and the mind staggers at the task of trying to count them; imagine them splashed and splattered over with all the earthly colors you ever saw and a lot of unearthly colors you never saw before; imagine them carved and fretted and scrolled into all shapes—tabernacles, pyramids, battleships, obelisks, Moorish palaces—the Moorish suggestion is especially pronounced both in coloring and in shapes—mountains, minarets, temples, turrets, castles, spires, domes, tents, tepees, wigwams, shafts."

—Irvin S. Cobb, Roughing It, Deluxe, 1913

21 Desert View

Desert View is the final stop on Desert View Drive. At 7,438 feet it's also one of the highest points on the South Rim. The top attraction here (other than the panoramic views) is Desert View Watchtower, designed by Mary Colter and built in 1932. Colter based Desert View Watchtower on the towers found at ancient pueblos in the Four Corners region. A circular staircase leads to the top of the 70-foot tower, which is decorated on the inside with reproductions of Ancestral Puebloan petroglyphs and depictions of Hopi legends. A gift shop is located inside the main building. Note: Because Desert View offers the only services in eastern Grand Canyon, it's a good place to fill up on gas and supplies.

"Days and weeks can be given to Desert View without exhausting the scene or the interest. You are away from the hotel and the crowd, and can see things like a lone eagle from your point of rock . . . the Canyon here is happily disposed for morning and evening effects because it runs practically east and west, and the light strikes not so much across it as along its length . . . One by one the tops of the buttes and points and promontories take up and carry on the light far down the Canyon. First one glows and shifts into a bright garb, and then another farther on repeats the litany of color."

—John C. Van Dyke, The Grand Canyon of the Colorado, 1920

Desert View Watchtower

22 Bright Angel Trail

SUMMARY

The Bright Angel Trail is the most popular trail in Grand Canyon—and with good reason. Starting near Bright Angel Lodge, this well-maintained trail descends to the Colorado River at the bottom of the Canyon, combining dramatic scenery with good footing and convenient facilities. Although strenuous, it's a reasonable hike for people of most ages and experience levels. A good choice for people without extensive hiking experience who are looking for a challenging hike.

TRAIL INFORMATION	BRIGHT ANGEL TRAIL
DISTANCE 15.6 miles round-trip	**DIFFICULTY** Strenuous
APPROXIMATE HIKING TIME 2–3 days	
TRAIL CONDITION Excellent, maintained	
WATER AVAILABILITY Piped in water seasonally available	
ELEVATION CHANGE 4,385 feet	

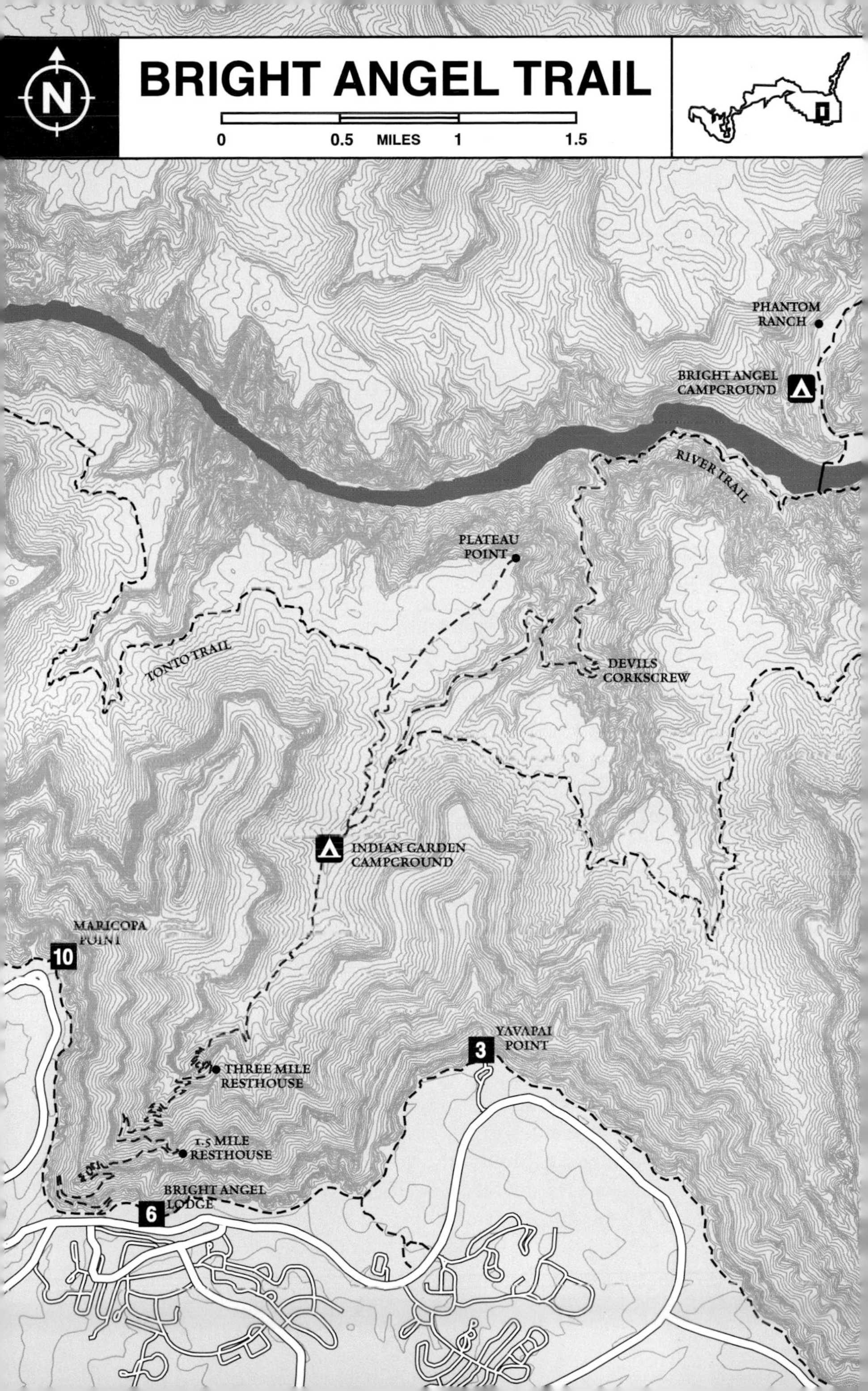

BRIGHT ANGEL TRAIL
N
0
0.5
MILES
1
1.5
PHANTOM RANCH
BRIGHT ANGEL CAMPGROUND
RIVER TRAIL
PLATEAU POINT
TONTO TRAIL
DEVILS CORKSCREW
INDIAN GARDEN CAMPGROUND
MARICOPA POINT
10
YAVAPAI POINT
3
THREE MILE RESTHOUSE
1.5 MILE RESTHOUSE
BRIGHT ANGEL LODGE
6

22 Bright Angel Trail

DAY HIKES

1.5 Mile Resthouse: 3 miles round-trip
2 Mile Corner: 4 miles round-trip
3 Mile Resthouse: 6 miles round-trip

PARKING

Parking is available in the parking lot a quarter mile south of Maswik Lodge or in the parking area just south of the railroad tracks near Bright Angel Lodge. Parking is also available at Lot E at the Backcountry Office east of Maswik Lodge.

TRAILHEAD

The trailhead starts next to Kolb Studio, near Bright Angel Lodge. The trail leaves the rim just to the west of the studio. A sign at the trailhead lists useful information such as temperatures, weather forecasts, and sunrise/sunset times.

NOTES

Mules are a common sight on the Bright Angel Trail. Even if you don't encounter a mule train, you'll undoubtedly notice their smelly leftovers on the trail.

TRAIL DESCRIPTION

After dropping below the rim, the trail immediately begins to zigzag across the canyon walls. You'll pass a small sign detailing the geologic layers you're about to pass through, and another sign warning you not to hike from the rim to the river and back in one day. This sign, featuring a particularly wretched-looking hiker, is repeated a few times along the trail, and is worth bearing in mind.

The trail, broad and well graded, creeps gently back and forth down the canyon wall. Soon, you'll come to a tunnel blasted through the Kaibab Limestone. Just past this tunnel, a collection of pictographs is visible above you to the left. These ancient drawings are believed to be the work of Havasupai Indians, but they may have been the work of an even earlier prehistoric culture.

The view spreading out in front of you is spectacular. Looking down the canyon, you can see the Bright Angel Trail snaking down through the Cottonwood trees that line Garden Creek. Farther along, stark and treeless Plateau Point is clearly bisected by the Plateau Point Trail (p.176).

After the Toroweap formation, you'll pass through a second tunnel. The trail then descends on switchbacks through the tan-colored Coconino sandstone and soon reaches the bright red Hermit Shale. A mile and a half from the start, the trail comes to 1.5 Mile Resthouse. This small hut, a good destination for a short day hike, offers good views and shade, as well as bathrooms, seasonal drinking water, and an emergency phone.

A quarter mile past 1.5 Mile Resthouse are some more impressive pictographs. Very easy to miss, they are on the underside of a triangular overhanging boulder

Jacobs Ladder

50 feet above the left of the trail. Red handprints, human figures, and other designs are visible.

Continuing along the trail, you'll soon reach the sign for 2 Mile Corner—2 miles from the rim and 2.5 miles from Indian Garden. The trail continues to work downward in irregular loops through the red rocks of the Supai Group. The next stop is 3 Mile Resthouse, a hut much like 1.5 Mile Resthouse but with better views. Water is available here (except in winter), but there are no toilets. There are a few small paths behind 3 Mile Resthouse that lead to pleasing and secluded views of the side canyon to the east.

Past 3 Mile Resthouse, the switchbacks grow shorter and shorter. This dramatic section, descending 500 feet through the Redwall formation, is known as Jacobs Ladder. After a series of rapid back-and-forth switchbacks, the trail meets Garden Creek and follows it down toward Indian Gardens.

The trail crosses the creek (which is sometimes dry) just before reaching Indian Gardens, passing by a ranger cabin and small medical station. From here the trail filters downhill through the cottonwoods to the campsites. Each campsite has a roofed picnic table, two boxes to store your food in, and T-Bars to hang your packs on. A bathroom and a water spigot are located a little uphill from the campsites. A spur trail to your left heads to the ranger station and the campsites, where there is a bathroom and water. The main Bright Angel Trail continues straight to the day use area, which also has bathrooms and water. There is a trail from the lower end of the campsite spur trail back to the main trail.

The Bright Angel Trail continues to the right of Garden Creek, while the west-bound Tonto Trail (which meets up with the Plateau Point trail) veers off to the

Secluded Cascade

left. Soon, the Bright Angel Trail passes by the pumphouse that brings water to the South Rim. Not long after, it reaches the eastbound junction of the Tonto Trail.

About a mile from Indian Gardens, the creek forms a small but beautiful cascade. Hidden by the narrow canyon that engulfs the creek, the cascade is easy to miss. About three quarters of a mile past the cascade, it is possible to scramble down to the creek and walk upstream to the cascade.

The trail descends to rejoin the level of the creek, crossing it twice before opening out above imposing Devils Corkscrew, a twisting 200-foot descent through the Vishnu Schist that loops back and forth across the canyon walls to the bottom of the canyon. Although the canyon walls provide some shade, Devils Corkscrew can be extremely hot in the summer. From the top, it switches back once and then curls around to the far side of the canyon wall. The trail then zigzags down to rejoin with Garden Creek.

The trail continues along the creek, crossing it twice, and soon reaches River Resthouse, a small hut with an emergency phone. At this point, the Bright Angel Trail officially ends and the River Trail begins. Follow the River Trail east as it runs above the Colorado River. After about a mile, the trail reaches Silver Bridge, one of two bridges that span the Colorado near Bright Angel Campground and Phantom Ranch. The second bridge, Black Bridge, lies a short distance upriver and can be reached by continuing along the River Trail. There are some Ancestral Puebloan ruins visible along the path between the two bridges on the north side of the river.

Once across the river, follow the trail to Bright Angel Campground and Phantom Ranch.

Devils Corkscrew

PLATEAU POINT

(3 miles round-trip from Bright Angel Trail)

Plateau Point, accessible via a spur trail near Indian Garden Campground, is one of the most beautiful viewpoints in Grand Canyon. A side trip to Plateau Point is highly recommended if you have the time.

The trail to Plateau Point is reached via the Tonto Trail. After crossing Garden Creek just below Indian Gardens, the Tonto Trail heads west and rises slowly as the creek descends to the right. The flat, clear path stays reasonably level as it winds along the contours of the western side of the Garden Creek sub-canyon. Another half mile brings you onto the plateau itself, which is completely exposed and shadeless. About three quarters of a mile from Indian Gardens there is a junction with the western branch of the Tonto Trail. Continuing on the Plateau Point Trail, you'll walk across the broad, flat platform for about a mile before reaching Plateau Point. The Point consists of a collection of Tapeats Sandstone slabs overlooking the Colorado River. A railing protects the outermost viewpoints, which provide tremendous views of the Colorado River. The plateau juts out far enough that the views to the east and west stretch on for miles. Sunset, the best time to go to Plateau Point, occurs earlier here than at most rim overlooks, but later than most other places within the canyon.

Plateau Point

23 South Kaibab Trail

SUMMARY

The South Kaibab Trail is the fastest, most direct route to the Colorado River from the South Rim. Many overnight hikers choose to descend the South Kaibab Trail, spend the night at Bright Angel Campground or Phantom Ranch, then return via the less demanding Bright Angel Trail. While most trails in Grand Canyon follow side canyons, the South Kaibab Trail follows open ridgelines, providing spectacular views of the inner Canyon.

TRAIL INFORMATION	SOUTH KAIBAB TRAIL
DISTANCE 13.8 miles round-trip	**DIFFICULTY** Strenuous
APPROXIMATE HIKING TIME 2 days	
TRAIL CONDITION Excellent, maintained	
WATER AVAILABILITY No water	
ELEVATION CHANGE 4,740 feet	

SOUTH KAIBAB TRAIL

23 South Kaibab Trail

DAY HIKES

Ohh-Ahh Point: 1.5 miles round-trip
Cedar Ridge: 3 miles round-trip
Skeleton Point: 6 miles round-trip
Tipoff: 9.2 miles round-trip
Panorama Point: 10 miles round-trip

PARKING

There is no parking near the South Kaibab trailhead. Hikers should take the free Hiker Shuttle or the Hiker Express.

TRAILHEAD

To get to the South Kaibab trailhead, take the free Hiker Shuttle that departs from the Green Line bus stop near the Grand Canyon Information Center. The shuttle will drop you off at the South Kaibab trailhead. There's also the Hiker Express that departs for the South Kaibab trailhead three times a day from the Backcountry Office.

NOTES

While not prohibitively difficult, the South Kaibab Trail has very little shade, no water sources, and no campgrounds between the trailhead and the river. Park rangers do not recommend ascending the trail during the sweltering summer months. While

most of the trail is exposed to the sun during the day, the walls of Yaki Point provide shade until about 10 a.m. in the summer for the first mile of the trail.

TRAIL DESCRIPTION

After heading to the right of the information board near the trailhead, you'll immediately drop down into a series of switchbacks running through the pale Kaibab Limestone. Once past the switchbacks, the trail runs gently downhill. The broad path and small walls on the sides of the trail make the steep drop into Pipe Creek Canyon much less intimidating. To the left, pinyon pines scatter across the slope. Bird watchers should keep their eyes out for scrub jays and mountain chickadees.

After a little under a mile the trail reaches Ooh-Ahh Point, a jumble of boulders with broad views across the canyon. Ooh-Ahh Point is a good stop for day hikers looking for a quick jaunt into the canyon, but there are even more impressive viewpoints further down the trail. Continuing on, the trail follows some switchbacks before turning the corner around Cedar Ridge and working its way along the crest of the ridgeline toward the Cedar Ridge viewpoint. There are bathrooms and a clearing here. This is one of the best day hike destinations on the trail.

After leading down along Cedar Ridge, the trail wraps around the east side of O'Neil Butte. From here you can see down into the dusty green bowl of Cremation Creek Canyon and the eastern Grand Canyon beyond. After roughly three miles, you leave the ridgeline and walk through a flat landscape dotted with cliffrose, mormon tea, saltbush, and yucca. Soon you'll reach Skeleton Point, an open viewpoint perched on a precipitous ledge. There is a misleading path to the left that

looks like it might be the trail, but the real trail descends to the right and quickly begins to switch back and forth down the steep slope.

Soon, you'll reach a sign indicating that you are 3.8 miles from Bright Angel Campground and 3.5 miles from the trailhead. The switchbacks continue unchanged for another half mile before flattening out. The trail heads to the north, passes the junctions for both the westbound and eastbound Tonto Trail, and then reaches the rim of the Inner Gorge. This area, known as the Tipoff, is a worthy destination for strong day hikers. Toilets and an emergency phone are located nearby.

Just past the Tipoff, the trail enters its steepest section, dropping roughly 1,600 feet in 1.7 miles. The path swings to the right before curling around and traversing to Panorama Point. Hidden deep in the Canyon, Panorama Point is the most impressive viewpoint on the trail.

Bending back to the right, the South Kaibab Trail drops into the black and pink heart of the Granite Gorge. Descending steadily, the trail loops east and then back west as it approaches a tunnel leading to Black Bridge. Fifty feet above the tunnel, the River Trail (linking the South Kaibab and Bright Angel trails) heads to the west.

The tunnel, blasted through the rock, is dark but short—flashlights or headlamps are not required. After crossing Black Bridge, head west along the north wall. Soon you'll see some impressive Ancestral Puebloan ruins to your left, marking the foundation of a large housing complex. Bright Angel Campground and Phantom Ranch are located farther along the path. If you're planning on spending a full day or two at Phantom Ranch or Bright Angel Campground, the Clear Creek Trail is an excellent day hike.

24 Hermit Trail

SUMMARY

The Hermit Trail, Grand Canyon's most popular unmaintained trail, is a rough but rewarding route from Hermits Rest, at the end of Hermit Road, to the Colorado River. Descending to the bottom of the Canyon in two steep drops, the Hermit Trail is hardly an easy path, but the views and sense of isolation make it one of the best trails in Grand Canyon.

TRAIL INFORMATION	HERMIT TRAIL
DISTANCE 18 miles round-trip	**DIFFICULTY** Strenuous
APPROXIMATE HIKING TIME 2–3 days	
TRAIL CONDITION Fair, unmaintained	
WATER AVAILABILITY Hermit Creek	
ELEVATION CHANGE 4,290 feet	

HERMIT TRAIL
N
0
0.5
MILES
1
1.5
HERMIT RAPIDS
WHITES BUTTE
TRAVERTINE CANYON
TONTO WEST TRAIL
CATHEDRAL STAIRS
YUMA POINT
BREEZY POINT
EREMITA MESA
HERMIT GORGE
PIMA POINT
14
BOUCHER TRAIL
HERMIT ROAD
HERMITS REST
15
SANTA MARIA SPRING
DRIPPING SPRINGS TRAIL

25 Hermit Trail

DAY HIKES

Waldron Trail Junction: 3 miles round-trip
Santa Maria Spring: 4.5 miles round-trip
Dripping Spring: 7 miles round-trip

PARKING

Overnight hikers can park next to the trailhead. Day hikers should park in one of the parking areas near Maswik Lodge or Bright Angel Lodge.

TRAILHEAD

Hermit Road, leading to the trailhead, is closed to the public. If you're camping overnight, however, you can open the gate to Hermit Road with the four-digit access code given to you with your backcountry pass. Drive seven miles to the end of the road, past the paved section, and down a short dirt road to the trailhead. If you're day hiking, take the Red Line shuttle that departs from the Hermit Rest Transfer, located about 200 meters west of the Bright Angel Lodge. You'll pass a number of viewpoints, such as Powell Point, Hopi Point, and the Abyss, which are good stops if you have the time.

NOTES

Parts of the Hermit Trail are fully exposed to the sun in the afternoon. Some hikers cache water on the upper sections of the Hermit Trail for the hike out. No camping is permitted above Hermit Creek Campsite.

TRAIL DESCRIPTION

The Hermit Trail departs from a warning sign on the left side of the parking lot. The Rim Trail's western terminus is also located here. The Hermit Trail runs through the woods at a moderate grade, eventually dropping out from the trees and traversing west for about a quarter mile. At this point the trail descends quite steeply—nearly 1,000 feet over the next mile. Although steep, the trail is well graded and sometimes paved with cobblestones.

As the trail descends, desert plants such as prickly pear cactus and agave start to appear. Three quarters of a mile down (a few switchbacks after the start of the cobblestones) there are some small prehistoric reptile tracks in the sandstone to the left of the trail. Soon after the tracks, the switchbacks become gentler, and the trail re-enters the trees. The Waldron Trail heads off to the left, and this junction is a good goal for many day hikers. The flat, breezy woodlands in this section make a pleasant and shady respite from the open switchbacks. After another quarter mile, the Dripping Springs Trail, another popular day hike, heads west from the main trail.

A half-mile past the Dripping Springs trailhead, you'll reach Santa Maria Springs. The spring itself is only a trickle clinging to the canyon wall, but that

trickle runs into a trough where you can replenish your water if absolutely necessary (the water is slightly foul and should be purified before drinking). Next to the spring is the Santa Maria Springs resthouse, a small three-walled hut with wild canyon grape vines providing shade on the western side.

From Santa Maria Spring, the Hermit Trail begins a long traverse through the Supai rock layers. The Supai traverse is dotted with rockfalls. The first few rockfalls, between Santa Maria Spring and the outlooks, are easy to manage, with a beaten path winding through the rocks. However, the rockfalls soon become larger and more difficult to negotiate. Several times you'll have to climb over and around unstable boulders. But patience is more important than strong route-finding skills. Occasionally, there are cairns marking the path of the trail, but don't be surprised to find fresh rockfalls where no trail markers exist.

For three miles past Santa Maria Spring the trail winds in and out with the contours of the land. The trail is nearly flat with sweeping views of the Canyon unfolding below. About a mile past Santa Maria Spring the trail reaches a small, unnamed viewpoint to the left. Continuing on, the trail descends some squiggly switchbacks and opens out onto a larger vista at Lookout Point, an arm of land jutting out about a tenth of a mile from the trail. Lookout Point is a good spot to rest and take in the view. Across Hermit Creek to the west you can see Yuma and Columbus Point.

The trail swings east after Lookout Point, following the curves of the rim as it bears northeast. After another mile, the path swings west to Breezy Point. Once again, the view is excellent, stretching down into Hermit Gorge and the Colorado River beyond. From here it's another half mile to Cathedral Stairs, a precipitous series of switchbacks that drop 500 feet to the desert scrub beneath the Canyon walls. After crossing a particularly tricky rockfall, the trail descends on switchbacks.

Although Cathedral Stairs descends a very steep face, the switchbacks themselves are not too difficult. Cobblestones appear on the trail again, and the trail's surface is generally well put together. Descending a notch between two towers of Redwall, the switchbacks increase in steepness until they reach a flat and gentle section of trail curving around to the northwest. Here the path continues for about a half mile above a talus slope. After Cathedral Stairs, the trail traverses steeply toward its final descent to Hermit Creek. Once past the switchbacks, the trail heads west for half a mile before reaching a junction with the Tonto Trail. The Tonto Trail runs east to west over much of the Grand Canyon below the South Rim. The Hermit Trail then follows the Tonto Trail west (left) to the campsite.

The trail runs three quarters of a mile from the junction to the campsite. A half mile from the junction, there is a good spur trail on the right that takes you straight down to Hermit Creek. Continuing along the main trail, you'll pass the abandoned ruins of the Santa Fe Railroad's Hermit Camp (p.152) before dropping down to the modern Hermit Creek Campsite.

The campsite contains several tent sites spread along and above Hermit Creek. Ammo boxes are provided to protect your food from wild critters. The creek is a good water source, but make sure to filter or purify the water before drinking it. Uphill from the creek is a solar toilet. Down the creek, just past the campsite, is a jewel of a mini-waterfall splashing into a small swimming hole.

The Hermit Trail continues down Hermit Creek for a mile and a half before reaching the Colorado. The trail is very beautiful, but difficult to follow. No longer a defined route, you'll have to pick your way along traces of the trail—some as good as new, some almost gone. The going is rarely tough, however, so you shouldn't have any trouble finding your way. Just follow the creek toward the Colorado.

Following the creek down from the campsite, the walls rise abruptly and soon the wooded creek bed becomes defined by stone slabs. A little farther on, the spur trail running down from the Tonto Trail reaches Hermit Creek. After meandering along, the creek straightens as it descends to the Colorado. A fallen slab soon appears that's as big as a house. At this point, the walls are 150 feet tall, and the trail continues through rocky banks and thickets as it heads toward the river.

Running along the stream, the trail enters a sandy area with some small trees before meeting the Colorado. If you're lucky, you'll catch a glimpse of excited river runners braving Hermit Rapids. Although you can camp by the rapids, the facilities are much better upstream.

If you're staying at Hermit Creek for more than a night, a day hike east along the Tonto Trail is a good option. The trail is very exposed to the sun, but Monument Creek, only two miles from the campsite, is a great destination. This beautiful streambed is relatively easy to follow up and down, but should be avoided if there is any threat of flash flooding.

25 Grandview Trail

SUMMARY

The Grandview Trail is a steep and beautiful path from Grandview Point to the top of Horseshoe Mesa, one of the few accessible "sky islands" (tall mesas) in Grand Canyon. The campsite on Horseshoe Mesa is a good destination for a hard day hike and a good base camp for exploring the surrounding area. Passing by the ruins of Last Chance Mine, the trail combines the stunning natural beauty of Grand Canyon with the rich history of its mining days.

TRAIL INFORMATION	GRANDVIEW TRAIL
DISTANCE 6.4 miles round-trip	**DIFFICULTY** Strenuous
APPROXIMATE HIKING TIME 2–3 days	
TRAIL CONDITION Good, maintained	
WATER AVAILABILITY Hance Creek, Miners Spring, Cottonwood Creek	
ELEVATION CHANGE 1,435 feet	

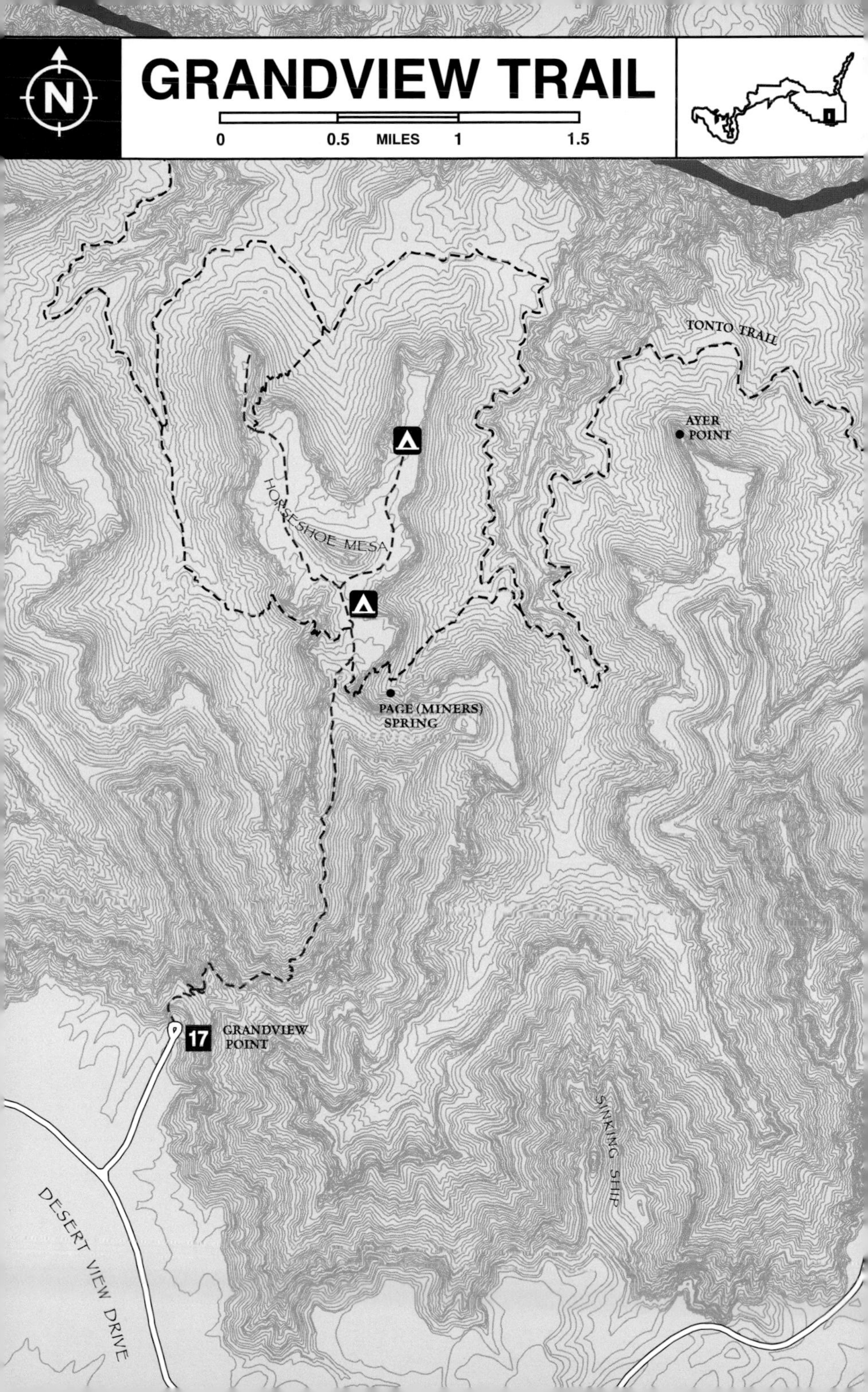

N
GRANDVIEW TRAIL
0
0.5
MILES
1
1.5
TONTO TRAIL
AYER POINT
HORSESHOE MESA
PAGE (MINERS) SPRING
17
GRANDVIEW POINT
SINKING SHIP
DESERT VIEW DRIVE

25 Grandview Trail

DAY HIKES

Coconino Saddle: 1.5 miles round-trip

PARKING

There is a parking lot next to the trailhead. The park service prefers that hikers use the upper parking lot at Grandview Point, leaving the lower lot for short-term visitors. Overnight hiker parking is located to the left of the main parking lot as you come in.

TRAILHEAD

To find the trailhead, head east on Desert View Drive away from Grand Canyon Village. After about 10 miles you'll see a sign marking the left turn to Grandview Point. There's a big parking lot with some toilet facilities and an information sign.

NOTES

There are no water sources near the campsite. All water must be brought in. If you hike the trail in the winter, use caution—the first mile of the trail can become particularly dangerous due to snow and ice. There are many abandoned mineshafts on the trial. Do not explore the mineshafts! They have been abandoned for decades and many are extremely dangerous.

TRAIL DESCRIPTION

The trail leaves from the information sign on the right-hand side of Grandview Point, then descends a series of steep, narrow switchbacks. Although the slope is steep, the footing is usually good as long as the trail is dry. After half a mile the grade becomes a little gentler as the trail zigzags through pinyon pine and juniper. There is a short side trail to the left of the viewpoint that leads out to a small platform with more great views of the Canyon.

The trail turns right at the viewpoint and descends steadily on cobblestones to Coconino Saddle, lying between a rock monolith and the rim. Coconino Saddle is a good destination for a short day hike. From the saddle, the trail traverses to the

MINING AND TOURISM

As you hike along the Grandview Trail, you'll undoubtedly notice metal cans and other trash left over from the days when Horseshoe Mesa was home to a productive copper mine. The copper mining operation on Horseshoe Mesa, run by Pete Berry, did well until the expense of transporting the ore up to the rim outweighed production costs. Pete Berry ultimately went into tourism and built a hotel at Grandview Point (p.160). The hotel is no longer there, but it was once one of the most popular destinations in the Canyon.

east, drops down into the trees, and switches back and forth for several hundred feet. As the trail approaches more open ground, the grade starts to level out. Although the trail is easy to follow, it can be quite rocky and rough.

Soon the trail passes an old mine shaft, the first of many in the Horseshoe Mesa area. The trail continues past the mineshaft and turns downhill toward Grandview Mesa. As the main trail continues, it crosses a junction with a trail leading to Cottonwood Creek and then passes Pete Berry's old cabin. The small cabin, roofless but still standing, contains some of Berry's old belongings and is worth a quick look. A spur trail near the cabin leads to the small group campsites and a toilet. The large group campsites are located farther down the main trail.

Two short trails run along the sides of Horseshoe Mesa. The shorter trail, which runs to the east, is roughly three quarters of a mile long. It passes through the two group campsites, over a small wash, and then works its way along the Horseshoe Mesa's rim. There are great views of Ayer Point, Miner's Spring Canyon, and the Colorado River to the east.

The second trail runs along the western arm of the plateau. About a mile in length, it swings left below the group campsites, runs west through a small boulder field, and then turns into a stand of junipers. The trail follows a wash for a short distance before becoming a real trail again and heading north. This side of the mesa soon turns into a narrow ridge that widens as the trail continues to the end. Although a route exists at the end that leads down to the Tonto Platform, the steep scramble is not recommended. If you want to visit the Tonto Platform, take the longer route down Cottonwood Creek.

THE COLORADO RIVER

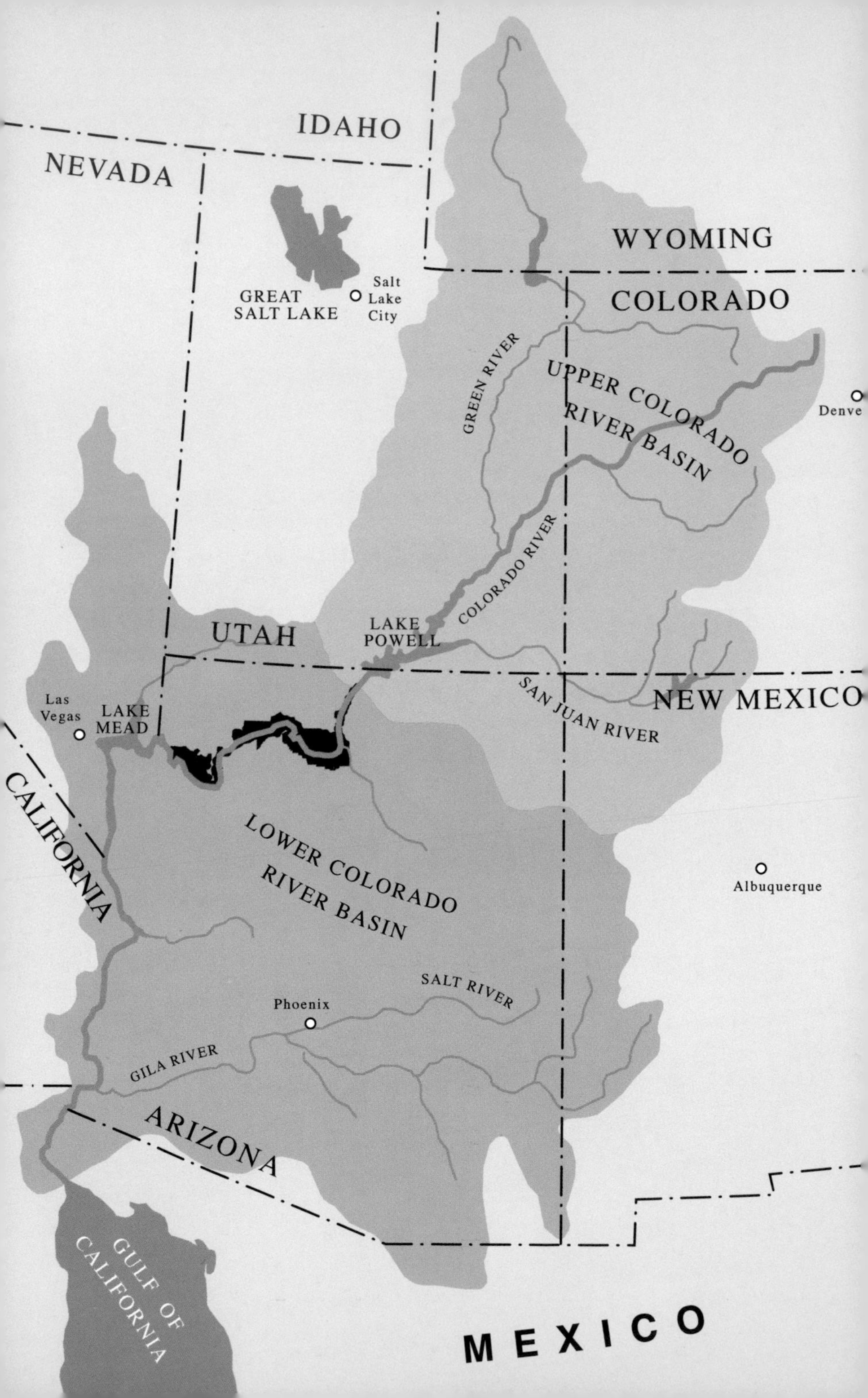
IDAHO
NEVADA
WYOMING
COLORADO
GREAT SALT LAKE
Salt Lake City
GREEN RIVER
UPPER COLORADO RIVER BASIN
Denve
COLORADO RIVER
UTAH
LAKE POWELL
SAN JUAN RIVER
NEW MEXICO
Las Vegas
LAKE MEAD
CALIFORNIA
LOWER COLORADO RIVER BASIN
Albuquerque
SALT RIVER
Phoenix
GILA RIVER
ARIZONA
GULF OF CALIFORNIA
MEXICO

THE COLORADO RIVER

The Colorado River is the heart and soul of Grand Canyon. Without it, there would be no Grand Canyon, just another quiet stretch of land rolling through northern Arizona. Instead, the river has cut a mile into the surrounding landscape, exposed nearly 2 billion years worth of Earth history, and flushed out over 1,000 cubic miles of eroded debris. The result is the single most impressive natural feature in North America.

As stunning as the view is from the rim, the view from the river is even more spectacular. Flowing downstream from Lees Ferry, just south of the Utah/Arizona border, the Colorado enters the most scenic stretch of whitewater in America. As the river cascades down a series of thrilling rapids, sheer cliffs rise up thousands of feet on either side, shutting out all reminders of civilization. Twisting deep into the heart of the Canyon, the river exposes a dazzling natural world. Towering rock formations shelter sandy beaches, dark caverns, and sparkling waterfalls. Labyrinth side canyons spread out for miles in all directions, channelling unlikely streams through the parched terrain. As the Colorado glides and swirls around sharp bends in the Canyon, cool shadows mingle with shimmering river light.

Only about 20,000 people, less than half of one percent of all park visitors, embark on a river trip through Grand Canyon each year—a number strictly limited by the park to preserve the pristine quality of the wilderness. Those lucky enough to witness Grand Canyon from the river are filled with an overpowering sense of awe. Physically, the size of Canyon is humbling. Visually, it's one of the most dynamic places in the world, changing with the weather, the seasons, and the particular time of day. Even seasoned world travelers admit that a river trip through Grand Canyon is one of the most remarkable journeys on the planet.

NATURAL HISTORY

FROM START TO finish, the Colorado River passes through some of the most beautiful and varied terrain in North America. Born in the deep gorges of the upper Rocky Mountains, it plunges head first down the pine-covered slopes to emerge in the desert Southwest. The river cuts through the wind-swept canyons of Utah, tears deep into the Grand Canyon, and then glides through the California desert. By the time it crosses the Mexican border to empty into the Gulf of California, the river has passed through seven western states and drained an area the size of Iraq.

The Colorado River is often referred to as the "Nile of America." At first glance, this comparison seems appropriate. Both rivers pass through vast desert regions and both sustain vast desert civilizations along the way. But despite these two basic similarities, the rivers share little else in common. In terms of size, the Colorado is a much smaller river, draining a quarter of the land that the Nile drains. In terms of length, the Colorado's 1,400 miles pales in comparison to the Nile's 4,000.

Even in America, the Colorado lacks many impressive statistics. It's not the longest river in America; six other rivers are longer. Nor is it the biggest river in America. In terms of annual flow, the Colorado doesn't even rank in the top 25. But what the Colorado does have, and what makes it so remarkable, is the wildest and most terrifying elevation drop of any river in North America.

From its headwaters in the Rocky Mountains to the Gulf of California, the Colorado drops over 13,000 vertical feet. This steep drop, occurring over a relatively short distance, churns up a river that is fast and furious, dropping an average of 7.7 feet per mile—25 times steeper than the mighty Mississippi. Because a river's erosive power increases exponentially with its speed, the Colorado would be a highly destructive river in any part of the world. But in the desert Southwest, a crumbling landscape filled with soft rocks and sparse vegetation, its erosive power is monumental.

As the Colorado enters the Southwest, it grinds away at the region's barren rocks, picking up tiny particles of sediment along the way. The more sediment the river picks up, the more abrasive it becomes. The more abrasive it becomes, the more sediment it picks up. This vicious cycle feeds on itself until the Colorado is, quite literally, a river of liquid sandpaper. Before massive dams plugged the Colorado, the river's sediment loads were phenomenal. Back then the Colorado carried an average of 235,000 tons of sediment through the Grand Canyon *each day*. "Too thick to drink, too thin to plow," was how one early explorer described it. The river's composition was often two parts sediment to one part water, and because the sediment had a high concentration of iron-oxide the virgin Colorado had a distinct reddish hue.

The virgin Colorado was also psychotically unpredictable. Early explorers often compared it to a bull. It was an "angry bull," a "blooded bull," and a "wild bull of destruction." The Colorado's flows in the Grand Canyon varied anywhere between 3,000 and 200,000 cubic feet per second (90 to 6,000,000 tons of water *per second*) sometimes within a matter of weeks. The largest flows occurred in the spring, when snowmelt from the Rocky Mountains set loose months of accumulated precipitation. In any given year, snowmelt accounts for over 70 percent of the river's flow.

The virgin Colorado's spring floods were biblical in proportion. Roaring through the Southwest, they ripped out vegetation, eroded huge chunks of the riverbank, and tumbled 20-ton boulders like ice cubes. During these floods the river carried its heaviest sediment loads, devouring the landscape at an astonishing rate.

But by winter the Colorado would slow to a trickle and hover just above freezing—a stark contrast to summertime highs when the river often topped 80

SEDIMENT LOAD

The amount of sediment a river can carry increases to the sixth power of its speed. A river flowing at 2 mph will carry 64 times more sediment (2^6=64) than a river flowing at 1 mph (1^6=1). Likewise, a river flowing at 10 mph will carry 1 *million* times more sediment than a river flowing at 1 mph. During spring floods the virgin Colorado flowed at speeds topping 40 mph, carrying up to 27 million tons of sediment through Grand Canyon *each day*. During these floods, Grand Canyon experienced its most intense erosion.

degrees. An entire ecosystem evolved to live in these harrowing conditions. The humpback chub, a fish found only in the Colorado, has a lifecycle timed to these wild temperature swings. It also has strong muscles and an uncanny sense of fluid dynamics to keep from washing away during the spring floods. Plants also adapted to the flooding. Apache plume, mesquite, and catclaw acacia grew only above the flood zone where they wouldn't be washed away.

As it travels to the sea, the Colorado passes through an amazing diversity of landscapes. In the Grand Canyon alone, it encounters three of North America's four deserts. Vegetation typical of the Great Basin Desert, found in Nevada and western Utah, is visible from Lees Ferry to river mile 39. From there, the river enters the northernmost outpost of the Sonoran Desert, covering much of Arizona, Southern California, and northern Mexico. At mile 157 the river enters the Mojave Desert, the smallest of the four deserts but home to such national treasures as Death Valley and Joshua Tree National Park.

The Colorado River in Grand Canyon is, on average, 300 feet wide and 25 feet deep. Within the Canyon the river is essentially a series of long pools interrupted by short, quick rapids. Although rapids only account for 10 percent of the Colorado's 277-mile length in Grand Canyon, they account for nearly half of its 2,000-foot elevation drop. The velocity of water in these rapids is up to 10 times greater than in the long pools in between. On most rivers, rapids form where the riverbed naturally drops, but in Grand Canyon rapids form next to side canyons. When flash floods roar through these side canyons, they dump debris into the Colorado. The debris constricts the river, backs it up, and creates a steep dropoff—the rapid. Some of these rapids drop up to 30 feet in a matter of seconds, and the most intense are considered among the most thrilling whitewater on the planet.

CERTAIN DEATH

IN 1849 an Indian who spoke no English attempted to describe the Colorado River to would-be river runner William Manly. Using a stick to draw in the sand, he mapped the upper Colorado passing through mountains, valleys, and canyons. He then piled up stones to represent the deepest canyon of all. According to Manly, the Indian, "stood with one foot on each side of his river and put his hands on the stones and then raised them as high as he could, making a continued e-e-e-e-e-e as long as his breath would last, pointed to the canoe and made signs with his hands how it would roll and pitch in the rapids and finally capsize and throw us all out. He then made signs of death to show us that it was a fatal place. I understood perfectly from this that below the valley where we now were was a terrible [canyon], much higher than any we had passed, and the rapids were not navigable with safety."

PSSI

THE NEW COLORADO

TODAY, GRAND CANYON is an oasis of uninterrupted whitewater on a river plugged with dams. Below Grand Canyon, Hoover Dam holds back Lake Mead, the largest man-made lake in the Western Hemisphere. Above Grand Canyon, Glen Canyon Dam holds back Lake Powell, the second largest man-made lake in the Western Hemisphere. Almost all of the water that enters Grand Canyon now passes through the turbines at Glen Canyon Dam, a fact that has significantly altered the downstream ecology.

Since the floodgates at Glen Canyon Dam closed in 1963, the Colorado River in Grand Canyon has undergone a dramatic transformation. Its flow, temperature, and sediment load—the defining characteristics of the river—have all changed. In fact, other than the path it follows, the new Colorado bears almost no resemblance to the pre-dam river.

The most obvious change has been to the river's flow. Historically, the amount of water flowing through Grand Canyon was determined by the amount of precipitation that fell on the Colorado River Basin. Today, the amount of water flowing through Grand Canyon is determined by the engineers at Glen Canyon Dam. Maximum flows are capped at less than 10 percent of what they once were, and the massive spring floods that created much of Grand Canyon have been eliminated.

This lack of flooding has created several problems. Most notably, much of the debris washed into the river through side canyons now lies dormant on the bottom of the river. Before the dam, spring floods cleared out the debris and washed it downstream. As a result, the Canyon is now filling up (albeit *very* slowly), and over time the rapids will grow worse and worse.

Although Glen Canyon Dam smoothed out the river's seasonal flows, daily flows became wildly erratic. The amount of water released from the dam is based on the region's fluctuating power demand, and during peak hours in the afternoon dam operators can charge twice as much for electricity as they can at night. When Glen Canyon Dam first opened, daily flows fluctuated anywhere

> Other than the path it follows, the new Colorado bears almost no resemblance to the pre-dam river.

between 3,000 and 31,500 cubic feet per second. Downstream, the river rose and fell like a toilet tank. Daily tides often topped 13 feet and beaches along the banks of the river eroded at an unnaturally high rate. In 1992 the Grand Canyon Protection Act was passed, requiring dam operators to smooth out releases to reduce their ecological impact.

Disappearing Beaches

Before Glen Canyon Dam was constructed north of Grand Canyon, the banks of the Colorado in Grand Canyon were lined with hundreds of sandy beaches. Deposited by the huge sediment loads of the virgin Colorado, these beaches provided valuable habitat for native species and were used as campsites by early river runners. Now that Glen Canyon Dam has reduced the river's sediment load by 80 percent, the beaches have started to erode. Many have disappeared entirely. The erratic releases from Glen Canyon Dam during its first several decades of operation significantly added to the problem. Timed to coincide with daily fluctuations in power demand, they created huge tides that stripped sand from the beaches and flushed it out of Grand Canyon.

Then, in 1992, President George Bush signed the Grand Canyon Protection Act, which ordered Glen Canyon Dam to operate in a way that protected and enhanced Grand Canyon National Park, including smoothing out daily releases. Maximum flows are now capped at 26,000 cubic feet per second (cfs), and daily fluctuations cannot exceed 8,000 cfs.

Scientists were convinced that smoothed out flows would significantly reduce the erosion of Grand Canyon's beaches. But to their dismay, beach erosion

continued at a steady rate. As it turned out, any new sediment brought into the Canyon by tributaries—theoretically enough to replenish the beaches—was languishing at the bottom of the river. What the Grand Canyon needed, scientists speculated, was a flood to stir up the sediment and redeposit it on the riverbank.

In March 1996 Secretary of the Interior Bruce Babbitt turned the wheel at Glen Canyon Dam to release a controlled flood of 45,000 cfs. The flood churned up the river and created more than 50 new beaches. Within a year, however, many of those beaches had disappeared. The flood, it turned out, didn't so much create new beaches as wash existing beaches further downstream. Some scientists blamed this failure on the timing of the controlled flood. The tributaries that bring new sediment into Grand Canyon do so mostly during the rainy summer season. By spring, when the controlled flood was released, much of this new sediment had already been washed out of Grand Canyon. In 2004 a second controlled flood was released in November, when sediment loads are much higher. The long-term effects of this flood are still being monitored.

The controlled floods, however, have stirred up just as much controversy as they have sediment. Each year every last drop of water in Lake Powell becomes more valuable than ever, and many oppose sacrificing this water to test unproven theories. But something needs to be done before the beaches disappear for good.

The dam also affects the Colorado's sediment load. Ninety percent of the sediment that used to enter Grand Canyon is now trapped behind Glen Canyon Dam, and each year Lake Powell fills up with more and more silt, a problem that future generations will have to contend with. In the meantime, water drawn from the downstream end of the lake enters Grand Canyon almost completely silt free.

The water released by Glen Canyon Dam, drawn from the chilly depths of Lake Powell, enters Grand Canyon at a constant 45 degrees. Not surprisingly, this frigid

The frigid water drawn from Lake Powell has significantly altered the downstream ecology of the Colorado.

water has significantly altered the Colorado's ecosystem. For millions of years fish native to the Colorado had their life cycles timed to the river's wild temperatures swings. They could survive in the cold winter water, but needed warm summer water to spawn. Now that warm water has disappeared from the Colorado, native fish have been forced to spawn in a handful of smaller tributaries.

As spawning grounds have disappeared, so have the fish. Of the canyon's eight native fish, five are now extinct. Among those lost is the impressive six-foot Colorado squawfish. The humpback chub, one of the few species that remains, has been pushed to the brink of extinction. Scientists estimate that there are fewer than 2,000 humpback chub left. Adding to the problem are non-native sport fish that have been introduced to the river. New arrivals such as trout, catfish, and carp thrive in the chilly water, and compete with native fish for resources.

But while the new Colorado has devastated native fish populations, it has allowed other life forms to thrive. The cool, clear water allows sunlight to penetrate its depths, fostering the growth of algae. The abundance of algae has formed the foundation of a healthy food chain and turned the river a gorgeous shade of green.

Even the riverbank has undergone a major ecological change. For millions of years the annual spring floods scoured the sides of the river. Now that flooding has been eliminated, a dense thicket of plants has taken up residence in the previous flood zone. This explosion of plants has led to a dramatic increase in animal habitat, and, consequentially, biodiversity.

Glen Canyon Dam completely changed the downstream ecology of the Colorado River. Although many conservationists would like to see the dam destroyed so the Colorado can be returned to its natural state, Glen Canyon Dam is unlikely to be decommissioned anytime soon. It provides valuable water and electricity to a region that is starved for both. And although the river's ecology has been shaken up, there have been many tangible improvements. The new river supports more plants and animals than the old one ever did, and its regulated flow allows hundreds of river trips to safely navigate Grand Canyon each year

HUMAN HISTORY

ALTHOUGH THE COLORADO River is often hard to see from the rim of Grand Canyon, the canyon itself is clearly visible from space. Equally impressive is the view from space at night when dense clusters of light appear in the surrounding desert. These are the booming cities of the Southwest. Over the past several decades, millions of people have flocked to cities like Phoenix, Tucson and Las Vegas, eager to leave cold winters elsewhere behind. This phenomenal migration, continuing today, would have been impossible without water from the Colorado River. In a land of little rain, the Colorado is a river of liquid gold that has allowed the Southwest to flourish.

Today, billions of dollars of agriculture, billions of dollars of industry, and millions of daily lives revolve around the Colorado River. Never before in history have so many people and such an enormous economy become so dependent on a single source of water. It is, without question, the most important natural resource in the West. But it is a limited resource, and huge demands have been placed on it. Today, its flow is so regulated and its water so overused that not a single drop reaches the sea. As the Southwest continues to grow, so do demands on the river. As a result, the Colorado has become one of the most argued over, litigated, politicized, and controversial river in the world.

The first attempt to tap the Colorado was a disaster. In the late 1800s, an enterprising developer named Charles Rockwood realized that, given a steady source of water, the California desert could be turned into an agricultural paradise. If the Colorado River could be tapped and controlled, farmers could grow crops an amazing 12 months of the year.

In 1901 a diversion channel was cut into the Colorado. Overnight, California's previously bone-dry Imperial Valley became one of the most productive agricultural regions on the planet. But because the Colorado ran thick with sediment, the diversion channel soon silted up and the Colorado jumped its banks, tearing off in a totally new direction. Instead of draining into the Gulf of California, the Colorado flowed into the middle of Southern California. For the next three years the river dumped its entire contents into the desert lowland area known as the Salton Sink. By the time engineers were able to redirect the river, an inland sea roughly one-third the size of Rhode Island had formed. The Salton Sea is still there today.

The Colorado was a force to be reckoned with, but there was too much money at stake to give up trying to tame it. The arid West was on the verge of a massive expansion, and savvy politicians realized that its future was linked directly to the water in its largest river. In the end, there was only one solution: build a massive dam that could regulate the Colorado, hold back its floods, and store them in a reservoir for later use.

In 1933 construction began on Hoover Dam. It was the biggest dam the world had ever seen. It tamed the Colorado, generated an enormous amount of electricity, and allowed the desert to bloom. Hoover Dam was such a resounding success that the government agency responsible for its creation, the Bureau of Reclamation, soon became the golden child of American politics. Using the momentum generated by Hoover Dam, the Bureau set off on a wild tear of dam building that lasted for the next 30 years.

The construction of so many expensive dams created huge economic windfalls in the states where they were built. With so much money at stake, dam building was politically charged across the country, but on the Colorado River the issue was even more complex. In 1922 a document called the Colorado River Compact had been drafted to allocate water from the Colorado River to the seven Colorado River Basin states. The Compact divided the region into an Upper Basin and a Lower Basin, each receiving 7.5 million acre feet of water per year. It was up to the states to figure out how to divvy up the water after that.

Not surprisingly, the Compact set off vicious inter-state water wars. Water was essential to each state's growth, and there simply wasn't enough to go around. The only way for a state to secure long-term water rights was to put that water to use before someone else did. The result was the hasty construction of massive multi-billion dollar irrigation projects that, in reality, made little practical sense. In a few short decades 19 dams had been built on the Colorado and its tributaries—many of them poorly conceived—and the river had been sucked dry.

Despite these problems, the Bureau of Reclamation continued to push for new dams. In 1963 Glen Canyon Dam was constructed to the furor of conservationists. When two more dams were proposed within the Grand Canyon itself, conservationists went wild. Led by David Brower of the Sierra Club, they used congressional hearings, letter writing campaigns, and modern media savvy to defeat the dams (p.101).

The Bureau's defeat in the Grand Canyon signaled a dramatic shift in popular opinion regarding dams. As the modern conservationist movement took hold, many citizens no longer viewed dams as glorious symbols of progress but as hulking symbols of man's interference with nature. This dramatic shift in public opinion soon brought the era of massive dam building to a halt.

The media blitz that defeated the dams also focused a tremendous amount of attention on the Colorado River in Grand Canyon. Soon, many ordinary people wanted to see it for themselves. Prior to 1950, fewer than 100 people had paddled through Grand Canyon. By 1970, 15,000 people were making the trip each year. To limit the river runners' ecological impact, the National Park Service began instituting strict rules and regulations. Today, roughly 20,000 people run the Colorado through Grand Canyon each year. And while the river as a whole is submerged in controversy, the uninterrupted stretch of whitewater in Grand Canyon remains one of the most rugged and beautiful places in the world.

THE COLORADO RIVER COMPACT

IN 1922 DELEGATES from seven western states gathered outside Santa Fe, New Mexico, to allocate water from the Colorado River. Their negotiations resulted in the Colorado River Compact. At the time, it was hailed as a "Constitution for the West." In reality, it was one of the most poorly conceived documents in the history of American politics.

The Compact "solved" the issue of water ownership by splitting the Colorado Basin into two: an Upper Basin (Utah, Wyoming, Colorado, New Mexico) and a Lower Basin (California, Arizona, Nevada). Of the estimated 17 million acre feet of water flowing through the Colorado each year, each basin would receive 7.5 million acre feet. Most of the rest went to Mexico. The Compact left it up to the states to decide how the water would be divided up after that. Not surprisingly, the Compact touched off vicious inter-state water wars. Tensions flared and relationships were bruised, but the worst was yet to come.

In 1953, the government admitted that there was a fatal flaw in the Colorado River Compact. The Compact had overestimated the river's annual flow by roughly 3 *million acre feet*. States that had fought tooth and nail over every last drop of the Colorado River were now faced with the gut wrenching fact that their figures were all wrong. The water rights wars were thrown into turmoil. They remain in turmoil to this day.

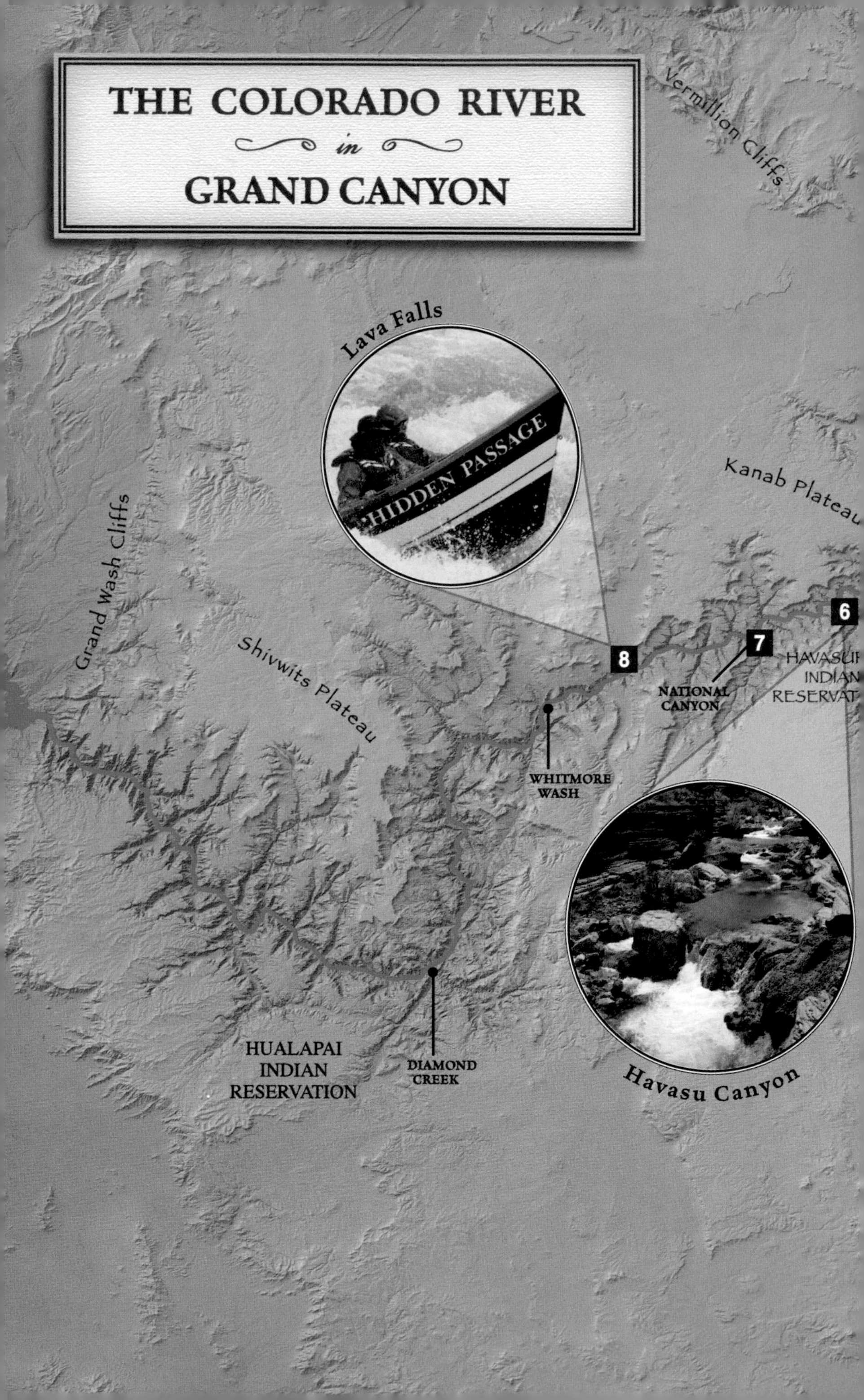
THE COLORADO RIVER
in
GRAND CANYON
Vermillion Cliffs
Lava Falls
HIDDEN PASSAGE
Kanab Plateau
Grand Wash Cliffs
Shivwits Plateau
8
7
6
NATIONAL CANYON
WHITMORE WASH
HUALAPAI INDIAN RESERVATION
DIAMOND CREEK
Havasu Canyon

Marble Canyon
LAKE POWELL
Paria River
1
GLEN CANYON DAM
2
LEES FERRY
Shinumo Creek
NAVAJO INDIAN RESERVATION
3
NORTH CANYON
Marble Canyon
KANAB CANYON
REDWALL CAVERN
SADDLE CANYON
BLACKTAIL CANYON
4
TRINITY CANYON
PHANTOM RANCH
BRIGHT ANGEL POINT
Nankoweap
GRAND CANYON VILLAGE
DESERT VIEW
LITTLE COLORADO RIVER
Coconino Plateau
Elves Chasm
Carbon Canyon
San Francisco Peaks

1 Glen Canyon Dam

This massive, 710-foot tall dam holds back Lake Powell 15 river miles north of Grand Canyon. Twenty-five feet thick and the crest and 300 feet thick at the base, it contains over 4.9 million cubic yards of cement. It took seven years to build and cost $272 million in 1963 dollars. If the dam's eight generators operated at full capacity, the dam would release 15 million gallons of water a minute and generate 1.3 million kilowatts of electricity.

Glen Canyon Dam went into operation in 1963. Since then, it has completely changed the characteristics of the Colorado River flowing through Grand Canyon. Water released from Glen Canyon Dam is drawn from the chilly depths of Lake Powell, and it enters Grand Canyon at a constant 47°F. Before the dam, river temperatures often topped 80°F in the summer. The new, frigid water has radically altered the downstream ecology (as well as the bathing habits of most river runners), and the filtering effect of Glen Canyon Dam has created a river that, unlike the pre-dam Colorado, is remarkably silt-free.

Conservationists loathe Glen Canyon Dam. In addition to the ecological changes it has wrought on the Colorado, the dam flooded Glen Canyon, by many accounts one of the most beautiful places in the Southwest. Supporters of the dam claim that Lake Powell is equally beautiful, and it allows motorboats to visit previously inaccessible reaches of Glen Canyon. In addition, the dam supplies water and power to region desperately starved for both.

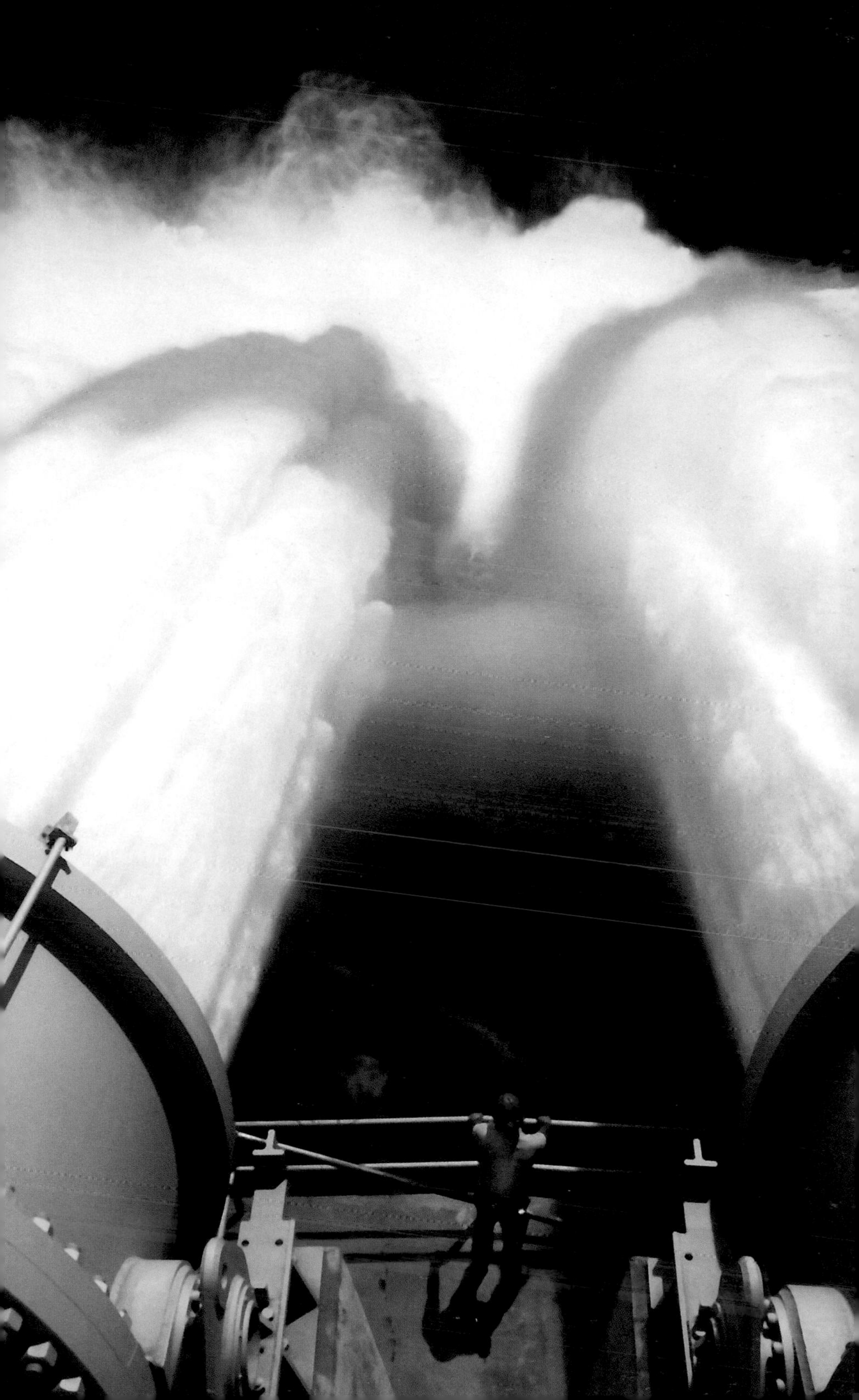

2 Lees Ferry (river mile 0)

Lees Ferry, Arizona is the first place north of Grand Canyon accessible by road. As a result, it's the launching point for every Grand Canyon river trip. (The next place on the Colorado accessible by road is Diamond Creek, 225 miles downstream.) Lees Ferry is also the official boundary between the Upper and Lower Colorado River Basins, a designation set forth in 1922 by the Colorado River Compact (p.211). The Compact essentially divided the Colorado's water between Upper Basin states (Utah, Colorado, Wyoming, New Mexico) and Lower Basin states (Arizona, California, Nevada). Implementing that deceptively simple plan, however, has proven to be a political nightmare.

In 1776 Fray Velez de Escalante, a Spanish priest who became the first white person to set eyes on Lees Ferry, wrote of this spot, "It has an agreeably confused appearance." Until 1929, when Navajo Bridge was constructed a few miles downstream, the agreeably confused Lees Ferry was the only practical river crossing for hundreds of miles. John D. Lee (p.91) was well aware of that fact when he established a ferry service here in 1872. Unfortunately for Lee, he was a convicted criminal on the run from the law, and shortly after he established Lees Ferry he was captured and executed. The ferry service continued to operate until 1928, when a ferry carrying a Model T capsized, killing all three people aboard.

3 Marble Canyon (river miles 0–61)

Marble Canyon gives river runners their first taste of the power and beauty of Grand Canyon. Its steep, narrow walls offer dramatic scenery broken up by dozens of exciting rapids. Ironically, there's no marble in Marble Canyon. The name was given by John Wesley Powell (p.87), who thought the sedimentary rocks, polished smooth by the muddy river water, resembled marble.

In the 1960s the U.S. Bureau of Reclamation wanted to build a dam at river mile 39. Had the dam been built, the upper reaches of Marble Canyon would have been flooded, but public pressure ultimately defeated the Bureau's plan (p.101).

"We have cut through the sandstones and limestones met in the upper part of the canyon, and through one great bed of marble a thousand feet in thickness. In this, great numbers of caves are hollowed out, and carvings are seen which suggest architectural forms, though on a scale so grand that architectural terms belittle them. As this great bed forms a distinctive feature of the canyon, we call it Marble Canyon."

—John Wesley Powell

OARS

"The water sweeps rapidly in this elbow of river, and has cut its way under the rock, excavating a vast half-circular chamber, which, if utilized for a theater, would give seating to 50,000 people. Objection might be raised against it, however, for at high water the floor is covered with a raging flood."

—John Wesley Powell

Redwall Cavern

YAMPA
HIDDEN PASSAGE

Carbon Canyon

Saddle Canyon

4 Nankoweap (river mile 53)

Many people consider Nankoweap to be the most beautiful place in Marble Canyon. In addition to spectacular scenery, this graceful bend in the river offers famous archaeological sites, pristine camping, and spectacular hiking nearby.

The origin of the name Nankoweap is a bit of a mystery. Some scholars claim the word is derived from a Paiute phrase meaning "Place Where Two Tribes Fought." Others trace its origins to a Paiute phrase meaning, "Place That Echoes." What is known is that Nankoweap was home to an Ancestral Puebloan settlement hundreds of years ago. These ancient people, predecessors of modern Indian tribes such as the Hopi and Navajo, farmed the fertile delta at Nankoweap and built granaries (stone storage compartments) in the cliffs above.

"And what a world of grandeur is spread before us! Below is the canyon through which the Colorado runs . . . Away to the west are lines of cliffs and ledges of rock—not such ledges as the reader may have seen where they quarryman splits his blocks, but ledges from which the gods might quarry mountains . . ."

—John Wesley Powell

Nankoweap

Trinity Canyon

Shinumo Creek

Granite Gorge

Elves Chasm

Blacktail Canyon

Deer Creek Falls

"The clouds are children of the heavens, and when they play among the rocks they lift them to the region above."
—John Wesley Powell
OARS

5 Kanab Canyon (river mile 143)

Kanab Canyon is one of Grand Canyon's largest and most beautiful side canyons. It was named by John Wesley Powell after the Paiute word for "willow."

Kanab Canyon is where Powell ended his second Colorado River expedition in 1872. Powell and his men hiked out of the canyon and headed to the nearest town. A year earlier, two men had discovered trace amounts of gold in Kanab Canyon, setting off a minor gold rush that brought hundreds of prospectors here. The gold rush lasted all of four months, ending when the would-be prospectors realized there was no more gold in Kanab Canyon.

"The crevices are usually narrow above and, by erosion of the streams, wider below, forming a network of caves, each cave having a narrow, winding skylight up through the rocks. Wherever we look there is but a wilderness of rocks—deep gorges where the rivers are lost below cliffs and towers and pinnacles, and ten thousand strangely carved forms in every direction . . ."

—John Wesley Powell

3 Havasu Canyon (river mile 157)

The beauty of Grand Canyon is stunning, but the beauty of Havasu Canyon seems almost hallucinatory. This secluded oasis—the most abundant side stream in Grand Canyon—is part tropical paradise, part Southwestern dreamscape. A well-worn path leads up the canyon from the river, revealing shockingly turquoise water tumbling over pink rocks in a series of tranquil pools, each one more beautiful than the last. No matter how far up the path you go, you'll be greeted with some of the most incredible scenery in the Southwest.

Havasu Canyon is located on the Havasupai Indian Reservation. Follow the path up the canyon 10 miles and you'll reach the village of Supai, home to about 400 Havasupai Indians. (*Havasupai*, loosely translated, means "People of the Blue Green Water.") Supai's world famous waterfalls draw thousands of visitors a year, but the village, located 2,000 feet below the rim, is only accessible by foot, mule or helicopter (p.298). It's virtually impossible to hike from the river to Supai and back in a single day, but Beaver Falls, located about four miles up the trail, is a beautiful waterfall that makes a good destination for strong day hikers.

Although Havasu Canyon only receives nine inches of rain a year, it drains a 3,000-square-mile basin. That drainage, combined with many springs, provides Havasu Creek with an average of 38 million gallons of water a day. The lurid blue of the water is due to a light coating of travertine (calcium carbonate leached from nearby rocks) on the riverbed, which gives the water its otherworldly hue.

7 National Canyon (river mile 166)

National Canyon is one of many exquisite side canyons branching off from the Colorado River. These canyons, carved out over millions of years by flash floods roaring down from the rim, offer some of the most amazing scenery in Grand Canyon. Their walls have been sculpted and polished in an endless variety of patterns, alternately catching and concealing the sunlight throughout the day. Many of these side canyons are accessible only from the river, making them the exclusive domain of river runners. Some go on for miles, offering incredible hiking that many river runners consider to be the best part of their trip.

"The gorge is black and narrow below, red and gray and flaring above, with crags and angular projections on the walls, which, cut in many places by side canyons, seem to be a vast wilderness of rocks . . . and ever as we go there is some new pinnacle or tower, some crag or peak, some distant view of the upper plateau, some strangely shaped rock, or some deep, narrow side canyon."

—John Wesley Powell

"What a conflict of water and fire there must have been here! Just imagine a river of molten rock running down into a river of melted snow. What a seething and boiling of the waters; what clouds of steam rolled into the heavens."

—John Wesley Powell

8 Lava Falls (river mile 179)

Lava Falls is one of the most challenging, terrifying and thrilling rapids in Grand Canyon. It drops 13 feet in a matter of seconds, providing a rip-roaring ride regardless of whether or not you stay inside your boat. Lava Falls is also proof positive of the Canyon's uncanny sense of drama: it's the last major rapid conquered on most river trips.

Lava Falls is named for the multiple lava flows that have occurred here over the past 2 million years, accounting for the dark-colored basalt on the north side of the river. Roughly 1.6 million years ago, a nearby volcanic eruption sent four cubic miles of lava tumbling down the rim. When the lava cooled, it plugged the Canyon and formed a dam at least 2,300 feet high. The dam created a reservoir that took 22 years to fill and stretched all the way back to Moab, Utah.

Lava Falls shows mercy to no man, as demonstrated in 1989 when the rapids flipped a boat carrying Hollywood heavyweights Tom Cruise, Jeffrey Katzenberg and Don Simpson. These Tinseltown titans were on a private "power trip" through Grand Canyon, popular among movie execs in the late 1980s. The luxury on these trips was so extravagant, so over the top, so beyond *anything* the Canyon had ever seen that they are still talked about to this day. As the moguls conquered the rapids, extra supply rafts tagged along carrying gourmet food, wine, white linens, fine china, assistants and private chefs. At night, candlelight dinners were served on the banks of the Colorado, featuring delicacies such as caviar, filet mignon, and live lobster.

THE NORTH RIM

★ ★ ★ ★ ★

THE NORTH RIM

ALTHOUGH THE NORTH RIM only lies 10 miles north of the South Rim as the crow flies, those of us confined to the ground have to drive 200 miles *around* Grand Canyon to get there. There's no question about it, the North Rim is remote. The closest major airport, Las Vegas' McCarran, is 280 miles to the southwest, and traveling to the North Rim means driving through one of the least densely populated places in the continental United States. As a result, fewer than one in ten Grand Canyon visitors ever makes it to the North Rim. But those who do are rewarded with some of Grand Canyon's most spectacular views—with one-tenth the crowds.

The North Rim is 1,000 feet higher than the South Rim, resulting in cooler temperatures and 60 percent more precipitation. The higher elevation also means the North Rim is covered in alpine forests of spruce, fir and aspen, giving it a feel more like the Rockies than the desert Southwest. During summer heat spells, when the South Rim is sweltering, the North Rim enjoys balmy afternoons and mild summer nights. Winters, on the other hand, bring so much snow that AZ-67—the only road to the North Rim—is forced to shut down. Only cross country skiers and snowshoers are allowed in the park during this time.

The hub of all activity on the North Rim is Grand Canyon Lodge (p.254), located at the southern terminus of AZ-67. The lodge offers overnight accommodations right on the rim, but even if you're not a guest you can relax on the open-air back porch or dine in the upscale restaurant, both of which offer spectacular Canyon views. A short distance away is the pristine North Rim Campground, which fills up fast in the summer. Both the lodge and the campground are located within walking distance of Bright Angel Point (p.257), the North Rim's most popular overlook, but a lazy drive along Cape Royal Road, which stretches across Wahalla Plateau to the east, will bring you to even more spectacular views at Cape Royal and Point Imperial (p.258).

Although the North Rim doesn't have much in the way of restaurants or gift shops, that's all part of its charm. Visitors here are more interested in the rugged scenery and multitude of day hikes along the rim. If you're looking for a challenging overnight hike, the North Kaibab Trail (p.280) descends 14 miles to Phantom Ranch. And if you're really looking to test your backpacking mettle, you can head 30 miles to the northwest to the exceptionally beautiful—and exceptionally challenging—Thunder River Trail (p.288), one of the best hikes in Grand Canyon.

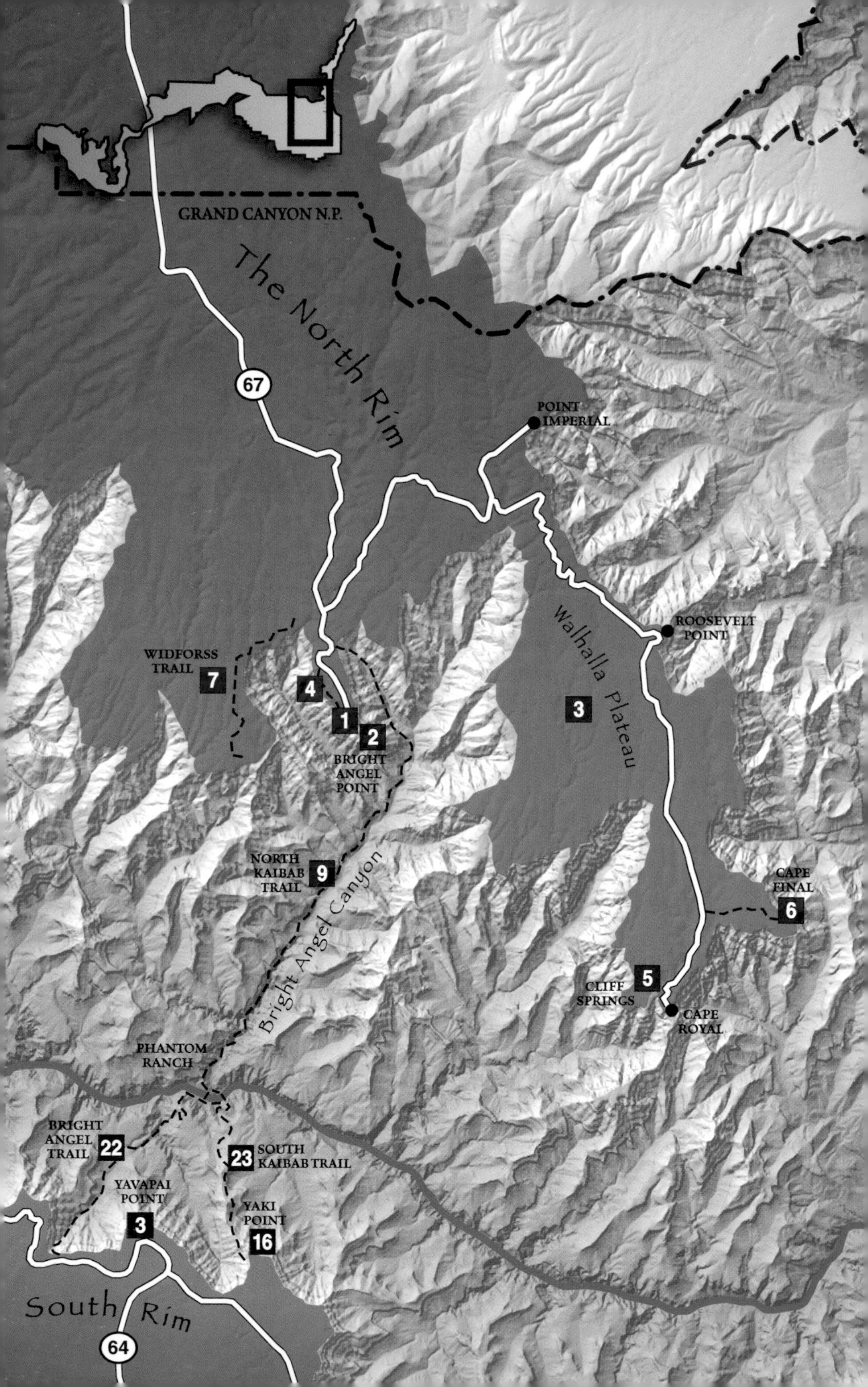
GRAND CANYON N.P.
The North Rim
67
POINT IMPERIAL
ROOSEVELT POINT
Walhalla Plateau
WIDFORSS TRAIL
7
4
1
2
3
BRIGHT ANGEL POINT
NORTH KAIBAB TRAIL
9
Bright Angel Canyon
CAPE FINAL
6
5
CLIFF SPRINGS
CAPE ROYAL
PHANTOM RANCH
BRIGHT ANGEL TRAIL
22
23
SOUTH KAIBAB TRAIL
YAVAPAI POINT
3
YAKI POINT
16
South Rim
64

North Rim BASICS

GETTING TO THE NORTH RIM

There's only one road to the North Rim: AZ-67, which heads south from the small town of Jacob Lake of I-89A. From Jacob Lake follow AZ-67 south 44 miles to Grand Canyon Lodge. No buses or trains run to the North Rim, but there is a trans-Canyon shuttle (see below). The closest major airports are located in Las Vegas, Nevada (280 miles distant) and Salt Lake City, Utah (380 miles distant).

RIM TO RIM SHUTTLE

From mid-May through mid-October, Trans Canyon Shuttle runs daily routes between the North Rim and the South Rim. The shuttle leaves the North Rim at 7 a.m. and arrives at the South Rim around noon. It then leaves the South Rim at 1:30 p.m. and arrives back at the North Rim around 6:30 p.m. Cost: $65 one-way, $120 round-trip. Reservations are necessary (928-638-2820).

INFORMATION

The best resource for North Rim information is the North Rim edition of the park's free newspaper, *The Guide*. Copies of *The Guide* are handed out at the park entrance station. Information is also available at the North Rim Visitor Center, located next to Grand Canyon Lodge.

WHEN TO GO

Summer is the busiest time on the North Rim, but crowds rarely get excessive. Fall brings changing leaves and crisp temperatures, making it one of the best times to visit. North Rim facilities shut down in mid-October, but the park remains open until winter's first heavy snow shuts down AZ-67 (anytime from October–December). In the winter the North Rim is open only to adventurous snowshoers and cross country skiers. The park reopens in the spring when the snow melts, but temperatures on the North Rim can stay chilly through June.

FEES

The North Rim entrance fee (which also gives you access to the South Rim), is $20 per vehicle or $10 per pedestrian, motorcycle rider, or cyclist. Admission is good for seven days. Another option is the National Parks Pass ($50), which gives you unlimited access to all U.S. national parks for one year.

WEATHER

Due to its high elevation, the North Rim is about 5–10° F cooler than the South Rim and receives significantly more precipitation. Afternoon showers are common in late summer, and deep winter snows can sometimes top 10 feet.

WHAT TO BRING

Warm clothes and rain gear are essential at any time of the year. A convenience store near the campground sells food and supplies, but selection is limited. Bring anything you need that you wouldn't be able to buy in a typical convenience store back home.

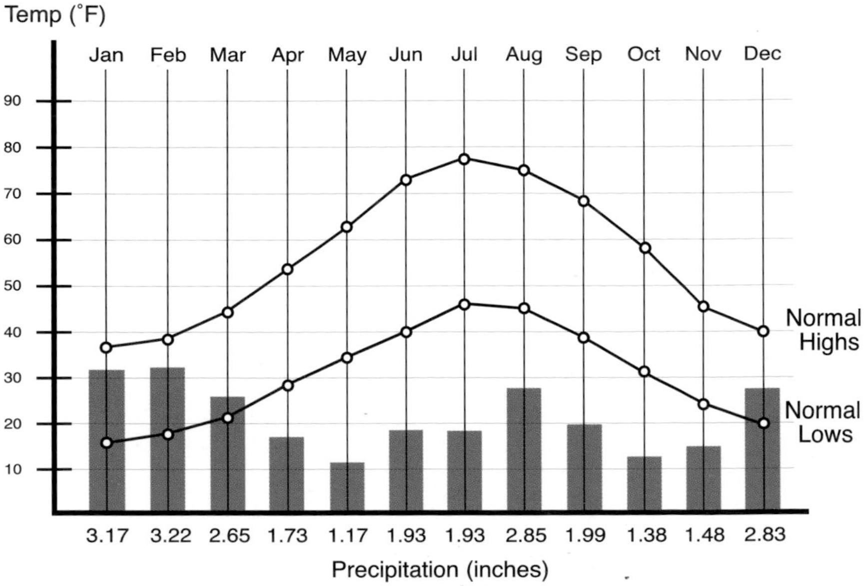

LODGING

GRAND CANYON LODGE

This rustic lodge, perched right on the rim of the Canyon, offers the only overnight lodging on the North Rim. Rooms are often booked months in advance during the summer, but same-day reservations due to cancellations are sometimes available (888-297-2757, www.grandcanyonnorthrim.com). Four types of rooms are offered: **Frontier Cabins** ($95) offer one double bed, one twin bed, 3/4 bath. **Pioneer Cabins** ($105) offer two bedrooms—one double bed, three twin beds—separated by 3/4 bath. **Western Cabins** ($115) offer two queen beds, full bathroom, and a porch; four cabins offer rim views ($130), but they are booked as much as two years in advance. **Motel Rooms** ($95) offer one queen bed and a full bath.

CAMPING

NORTH RIM CAMPGROUND

This pristine campground, located about a mile northwest of Grand Canyon Lodge, has 87 sites, four with Canyon views. Rate: $15 ($20 for the four sites with Canyon views); backpackers and other visitors without cars only pay $4 per night. Reservations are highly recommended (800-365-2267, www.reservations.nps.gov).

GETTING AROUND THE NORTH RIM

BY CAR

If you plan on exploring any part of the North Rim not within walking distance of Grand Canyon Lodge (Point Imperial Road, Cape Royal Road), having your own car is essential.

BY SHUTTLE

The North Rim Hiker Shuttle runs between Grand Canyon Lodge and the North Kaibab Trailhead. Cost: $5 for the first person, $2 each additional person. Departs 5:20 a.m. and 7:20 a.m. daily. Tickets available at Grand Canyon Lodge's front desk.

ON FOOT

There are several trails and overlooks within walking distance of Grand Canyon Lodge. Exploring the rest of the North Rim on foot is not practical.

BY BICYCLE

Bikes are allowed on all paved and dirt roads on the North Rim, unless otherwise posted. They are prohibited from all other park trails.

DINING

GRAND CANYON LODGE DINING ROOM

Offers fine dining on the North Rim with tremendous views of the Canyon. Open for breakfast, lunch and dinner. Dinner reservations required (928-638-2612).

CAFE ON THE RIM

A cafeteria located on the west side of Grand Canyon Lodge. Open 7 a.m.–9 p.m.

ROUGH RIDER SALOON

Coffee shop by day, well-stocked bar by night. Located on the east side of Grand Canyon Lodge. Open 5 a.m.–9 a.m., 11 a.m.–10 p.m.

SERVICES

NORTH RIM GENERAL STORE

Located near the entrance to the North Rim Campground. Offers basic groceries and camping supplies. Open 8 a.m.–8 p.m., but hours can vary with demand.

GAS

There's a small gas station on the road to the North Rim Campground, off AZ-67 north of Grand Canyon Lodge. Open 7 a.m.–7 p.m. daily.

POST OFFICE

Located in Grand Canyon Lodge. Open Monday–Friday.

LAUNDRY & SHOWERS

Coin-operated laundry and showers are located near the entrance to the North Rim Campground. Open 7 a.m.–7 p.m. daily.

ENTERTAINMENT

RANGER PROGRAMS

Free ranger programs are offered on topics including history, geology, wildlife and more. Highly recommended. Check *The Guide* for exact times and locations.

MULE TRIPS

Day trips are offered along the rim and partway down the North Kaibab Trail. One-hour trips ($30), half-day trips ($55), and full-day trips ($105, including lunch) are offered. For more information visit the Grand Canyon Trail Rides desk at Grand Canyon Lodge (435-679-8665).

Jacob Lake BASICS

Jacob Lake, a tiny town 44 miles north of Grand Canyon Lodge, and AZ-67 are home to a handful of shops, lodges and restaurants. When winter snow closes AZ-67, everything but the Jacob Lake Inn shuts down until the following spring. The Kaibab Plateau Visitor Center (928-643-7298), located near the junction of 89-A and AZ-67, offers information and exhibits on the surrounding area.

LODGING

JACOB LAKE INN

Offers motel rooms ($95), cabins ($75–$120) and family units that sleep up to six ($120). Open year-round (928-643-7232, www.jacoblake.com).

KAIBAB LODGE

Offers rustic cabins that sleep up to eight. Located 26 miles south of Jacob Lake. **Rates**: $85–200 (928-638-2389, www.kaibablodge.com).

CAMPING

DEMOTTE PARK CAMPGROUND

Located next to the Kaibab Lodge. Open June–September. Rate: $10 per vehicle, no reservations (800-525-0924, www.canyoneers.com).

JACOB LAKE CAMPGROUND

Located just west of the junction of 89-A and AZ-67. Offers tent camping sites mid-May–October. **Rate**: $10 per vehicle, no reservations (928-643-7770).

KAIBAB CAMPER VILLAGE

Offers tent sites ($15) and RV sites with hook-ups ($30). Open mid-May through mid-October. Reservations available (928-643-7804, www.kaibabcampervillage.com).

1 Grand Canyon Lodge

Grand Canyon Lodge is the first stop for most visitors to the North Rim. Perched right on the rim, not far from Bright Angel Point, it offers tremendous views of the Canyon from its two bench-filled, open-air terraces. During the day, these terraces are a great place to relax and take in the views; at night a crackling fire is often built in the stone fireplace on the eastern terrace. Sandwiched between the terraces is the indoor Sun Room, where comfy leather chairs face giant picture windows. And just up the steps from the Sun Room is the Grand Canyon Lodge Dining Room, an upscale restaurant that, not surprisingly, also features giant picture windows with spectacular views.

The original Grand Canyon Lodge was built in 1928. At the time, Stephen Mather, the director of the National Park Service, was championing the construction of grand lodges in then-remote western parks to help lure visitors. Designed by Gilbert Stanley Underwood (the man behind Yosemite's famous Ahwahnee Hotel), the original Grand Canyon Lodge was built out of native ponderosa pines and Kaibab limestone. But just four years after it opened, an accidental fire burned down the original structure. (The small buildings on either side of the structure, however, were spared, and they are still in use today.) The current lodge was built in 1936. When it was finished it boasted improvements such as steel beams (as opposed to flammable pine beams) and sloped roofs to deflect the North Rim's heavy snows.

2 Bright Angel Point

This popular viewpoint, located southeast of Grand Canyon Lodge, is accessible via a short, paved path that begins to the left of the North Rim Visitor Center, just beyond the cabin area. After an initial drop at the start, the trail stays relatively flat with only a few mild ups and downs. Dramatic views of Roaring Springs Canyon unfold to your left, and towards the end of the trail you'll come to a small bridge that takes you to Bright Angel Point. The point itself is fenced in by a small metal railing, and interpretive signs point out famous Canyon landmarks visible from Bright Angel Point. The rocky outcrop directly behind the observation platform is a popular place to take in the view, but if you choose to climb onto the overlook be extremely careful of the sheer drop-offs.

In the distance, the South Rim appears as a sheer wall on the far side of the Canyon. Because both sides of Grand Canyon are tilted slightly to the south, precipitation that falls on the North Rim flows *into* the Canyon while precipitation that falls on the South Rim flows *away* from the Canyon. Because the walls of the North Rim receive so much more runoff, they have eroded horizontally up to 10 times faster than the walls of the South Rim. As a result, the walls of the North Rim gradually recede back from the river while the walls of the South Rim appear nearly vertical.

Beyond the South Rim are the San Francisco Mountains. On clear days you can make out Humphrey's Peak, the highest point in Arizona at 12,643 feet.

3 Walhalla Plateau

This dramatic plateau, jutting out 15 miles into the Canyon just east of Bright Angel Point, contains some of the North Rim's finest and most accessible viewpoints. To get there by car from Grand Canyon Lodge, drive north three miles on AZ-67 and turn right onto Fuller Canyon Road. Soon the road forks; heading left takes you to Point Imperial, heading right takes you to Cape Royal.

Head left at the fork and you'll drive about three miles to Point Imperial. At 8,803 feet, Point Imperial is the highest vantage point on either rim. The dramatic spire to the east marks the top of Mount Hayden.

Head right at the fork and you'll follow 16-mile Cape Royal Road to the southern tip of Walhalla Plateau. Along the way you'll pass a number of worthwhile viewpoints including Vista Encantada, which has picnic tables, and Roosevelt Point, which provides a rare glimpse of the confluence of the Colorado and Little Colorado Rivers. Cape Final (p.268) is a short, highly recommended day hike that starts six miles past Roosevelt Point. Continuing on, the road passes Walhalla Overlook. Across the road from the overlook are the remains of a six-room Ancestral Puebloan pueblo, thought to have been inhabited around A.D. 1050.

A large parking area marks the end of Cape Royal Road. From the parking area a short, paved trail passes by Angel's Arch—a natural arch that frames a view of the Colorado—en route to Cape Royal, the southernmost viewpoint on the North Rim, which provides sweeping views of the Canyon.

4 Transept Trail

SUMMARY
The Transept Trail, which connects Grand Canyon Lodge with the North Rim Campground, is a charming stroll along the dramatic edge of Transept Canyon. This easy path offers great views and frequent wildlife sightings in the morning and evening.

TRAIL INFORMATION	TRANSEPT TRAIL
DISTANCE 3 miles round-trip	**DIFFICULTY** Easy
APPROXIMATE HIKING TIME 1.5 hours	
TRAIL CONDITION Good, maintained	
WATER AVAILABILITY No water	
ELEVATION CHANGE 100 feet	

TRANSEPT TRAIL

0 .33 MILES .66 1

4 Transept Trail

PARKING

Parking is available at the North Rim Campground and Grand Canyon Lodge.

TRAILHEAD

The Transept Trail runs between the North Rim Campground and Grand Canyon Lodge. The campground trailhead starts just west of the general store; a sign marks the trail. (To follow the trail from Grand Canyon Lodge, start the Bright Angel Point Trail and turn right off of the pavement after one-tenth of a mile.)

TRAIL DESCRIPTION

From the campground: The trail is broad and flat as it leaves the campground. For the first third of a mile, the campground remains visible through the trees on the left. Soon, several fine viewpoints appear on the right. The trail's namesake, the Transept, is the massive rock outcrop on the opposite side of Transept Canyon, which drops down to the right of the trail. The Transept is distinguished by its pale top layer and brick red bottom. Beyond Transept Canyon you can see Brahma, Deva and Zoroaster Temples in the main body of Grand Canyon.

As the trail continues, you'll see several small side trails that lead out and back from the main trail. These trails are rugged and unmaintained and some lead to dangerous viewpoints. Use caution if you choose to explore these trails.

As the main trail continues, it turns left into a woody grove filled with aspens and ponderosa pines that open up occasionally on dramatic canyon views. The trail then follows the contours of the nearby streambeds, sometimes crossing over them on small bridges.

Wildlife is a common sight on the Transept Trail. Among the most frequently spotted animals are mule deer, chipmunks, and squirrels. Birdwatchers should keep an eye out for wrens, juncos and woodpeckers. The density of animals here is the result of the trail's close proximity to both the campground and the lodge. The animals are drawn to the food that people accidentally leave behind. Note: Feeding animals is illegal; rangers will ticket you.

As the trail continues, it passes a small Ancestral Puebloan ruin, then veers left toward a large outlook on a little shoulder of land. Benches are set up here from which you can see Bright Angel Point, Bright Angel Canyon, and the Temples beyond. Farther down the trail you may see several burnt-out trees. As with many North Rim trails, the Transept was swept by fire and retains some damage.

The trail gradually rises back toward the rim, passing the cabins of the Grand Canyon Lodge on the left. Eventually, the trail leads back to the lodge itself. There are more outlooks to your right, several of which stretch out on precipitous tongues of rock. The trail continues through shaded stretches of tall trees and sunny open sections, eventually passing by the front of the lodge. The trail ultimately merges with the pavement of the Bright Angel Point Trail.

5 Cliff Spring Trail

SUMMARY
Cliff Spring Trail brings hikers through a woody glade to a tranquil spring. While not particularly challenging, the trail does have some marked rises and falls, as well as some steep drop-offs if the trail is followed to the end.

TRAIL INFORMATION	CLIFF SPRING TRAIL
DISTANCE 1–2 miles round-trip	**DIFFICULTY** Easy
APPROXIMATE HIKING TIME Up to 1 hour	
TRAIL CONDITION Good, unmaintained	
WATER AVAILABILITY Cliff Spring (requires treatment)	
ELEVATION CHANGE 200 feet	

CLIFF SPRING

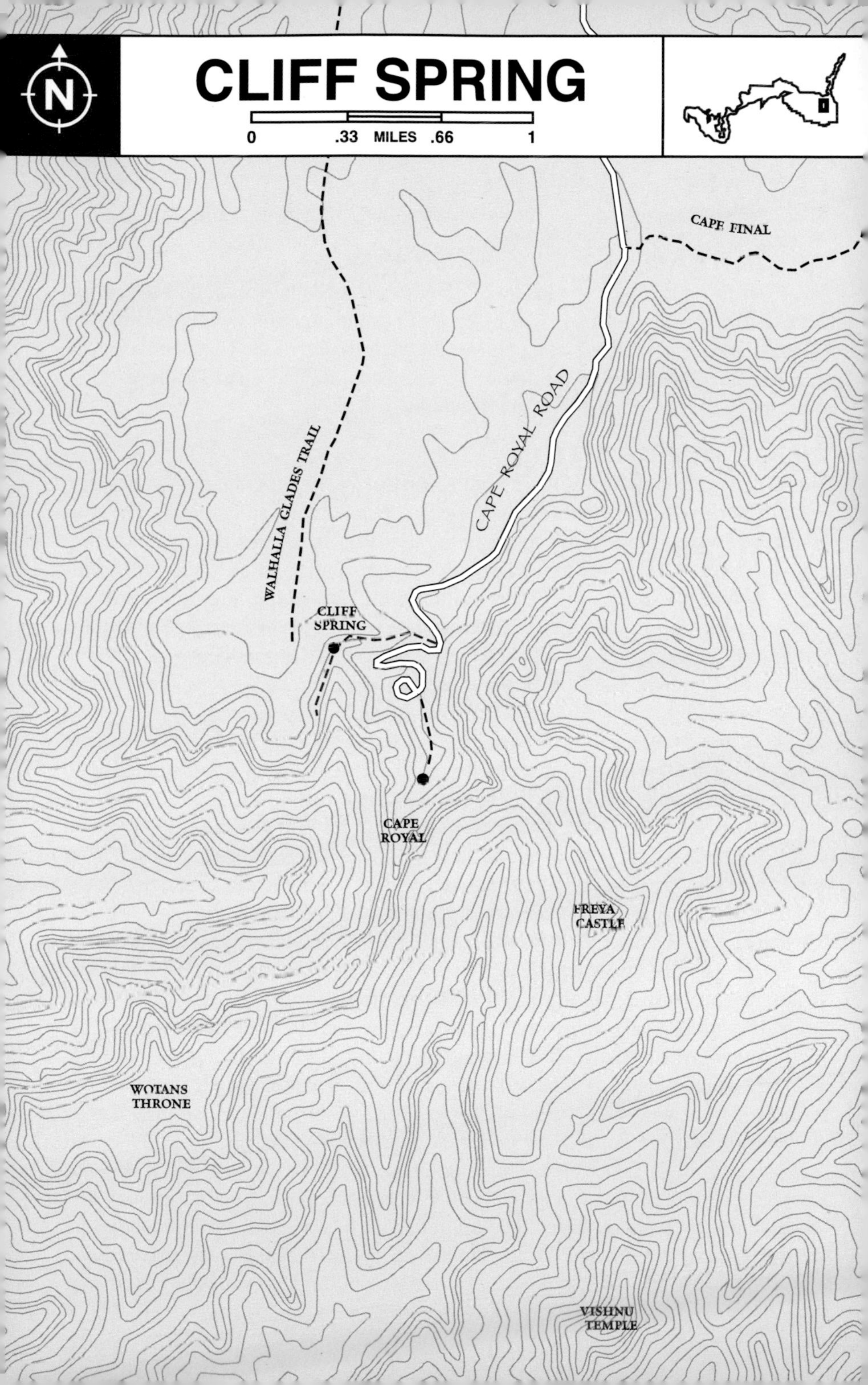

5 Cliff Spring Trail

PARKING

There is a parking area across the street from the Cliff Spring trailhead.

TRAILHEAD

The Cliff Spring Trail starts inside of a hairpin right-hand turn a half mile from the end of Cape Royal Road (13.7 miles south of the junction with Point Imperial Road). Parking is available at a pullover on the left side of the road, and a signed trailhead is located across the street. The well-maintained dirt trail drops down from the road into a forest of ponderosa pines.

TRAIL DESCRIPTION

Shortly after the trail begins there is an Ancestral Puebloan granary to your right, used in ancient times to store crops such as beans, corn and squash. The trail continues to slope downward, running parallel to a creek bed on the left before crossing over it. It curves around a large boulder and through a pleasant mini-valley before re-crossing the creek. As the trail continues, it hugs some striking 30-foot cliffs with a pronounced overhang. The trail bends to the right and flattens out next to the plummeting creek bed, where what was a dip suddenly becomes its own narrow canyon. The Cliff Spring Trail continues above the tops of evergreen trees, sheltered in the side of a pale sandstone wall.

Soon, the small clumps of vegetation clinging to the canyon walls become thick and mossy. Fern-like thistles spring up to the right. There is a dripping sound here, and you can see Cliff Spring squeezing itself out of the rock. Because this is a constant source of water, it is an excellent place for bird watching. Violet-green swallows, rock wrens, and ravens all nest nearby. There is a large flat rock from which you can gaze out into the depths of the canyon. In the distance you can see Wotan's Throne rising perpendicular to Cape Royal and Cliff Spring.

The cliff marks the end of the maintained Cliff Springs Trail, but a rugged path continues a half mile farther, curling left toward the southern tip of the Walhalla Plateau. This unofficial trail leads straight from the spring and turns sharply left after a tenth of a mile. The awning-style overhang lowers, the trail narrows, and the footing becomes more rugged. The small dirt path hugs the cliff and the overhang becomes quite low. This part ends quickly, however, and the rugged path continues on. Cape Royal will soon appear on the left across the canyon. The going here is quite rough, but the trail is easy to see. A quarter mile from the spring, the trail looks as if it might climb up a steep slope to a saddle in the cliff, but it doesn't. Instead, the route continues to hug the cliff face, but remains separate enough that the gigantic rock and boulder formations are easily visible overhead. Curling around the end of Walhalla Plateau, the trail heads closer to the cliffs, slopes down a little, and ends in a flat section of red sandstone. From here you can retrace your steps back to Cliff Spring.

6 Cape Final Trail

SUMMARY

The Cape Final Trail runs through cool, open woodlands to a dramatic and uncrowded eastern vista. A spectacular day hike, this trail is also an excellent short camping trip that can be accomplished by almost anyone who can carry a backpack.

☆ *Highly Recommended*

TRAIL INFORMATION	CAPE FINAL TRAIL
DISTANCE 4 miles round-trip	**DIFFICULTY** Easy
APPROXIMATE HIKING TIME 2 hours	
TRAIL CONDITION Good, rehabilitated dirt road	
WATER AVAILABILITY No water	
ELEVATION CHANGE 150 feet	

N
CAPE FINAL
0
.5
MILES
1
1.5
GUNTHER CASTLE
SIEGFRIE PYRE
FRANCOIS MATTHES TRAIL
CAPE ROYAL ROAD
NAJI POINT
NATCHI CANYON
WALHALLA GLADES TRAIL
JUNO TEMPLE
CAPE FINAL
JUPITER TEMPLE
VENUS TEMPLE
CAPE ROYAL
APOLLO TEMPLE
FREYA CASTLE
BASALT CLIFFS
WOTANS THRONE
VISHNU TEMPLE
KRISHNA SHRINE
RAMA SHRINE

6 Cape Final Trail

PARKING

There is a parking area next to the trailhead.

TRAILHEAD

From Grand Canyon Lodge, drive north on AZ-67 and turn right on Cape Royal/ Point Imperial Road. Drive 5.4 miles until you reach a "Y" junction. Bear right toward Cape Royal. After about 15 miles, a sandy parking area will appear on your left. The trail leads to the left of the parking area into the stately forest of ponderosa pines.

NOTES

It is possible to camp at Cape Final. The Backcountry Office gives out one camping permit per night, so if you have one, you will have Cape Final all to yourself! Cape Final itself can be a bit hard to find. Look for USGS datum points embedded in the bedrock at the overlook.

TRAIL DESCRIPTION

The trail rises slightly at the start with the land sloping down a little on either side. The trail is dirt with a few rocks, but flat and broad enough for two people with backpacks to walk shoulder to shoulder. Pay no attention to the occasional diamond-shaped pieces of tin nailed to trees. They were once used as trail markers when snow covered the trail, but at present they are disused and unnecessary.

As you walk, the edge on your right-hand side begins to come closer. Soon, you can catch a glimpse of the Canyon's rim to your right through the trees. After another half mile the upward grade ends and the trail flattens out of its gentle climb, curving gradually to the right and undulating a bit up and down. As you meander through the pines, the land on either side begins to narrow. Eventually you'll cross a small creek bed. The trail continues for another mile as you approach the edge of the woods.

At this point a small side trail goes left to the first overlook, a dramatic drop to the east. The overlook's sudden red emptiness comes as a wonder and a shock after walking through the forest. From here the trail narrows but remains good, rolling along parallel to the spit of land that you're following. There is another equally impressive viewpoint a short distance later. The trail then turns to the right and winds through the woods as the peninsula you're on grows narrower and narrower.

Continuing along, the trail plunges left into the scrub and the vegetation begins to get a little more desert-like as cacti and pinyon pines replace ponderosas. The trail drops sharply for 50 feet, then returns to its normal flat grade. Soon you'll reach the clearly marked Cape Final side trail. This trail winds through low cacti and scrub (climbing some white rocks that may require your hands to steady you) before opening out onto a spectacular view of the eastern canyon.

In front of you, Jupiter Temple and Juno Temple rise in a fin-like ridge. To the left, you can see the towering Siegfried Pyre, with Hubbell Butte and Chiavria Point extending from it to the south. To your right, you see the pyramids of Vishnu Temple and Rama Shrine, with Krishna Shrine just in sight to the far right. The Unkar Creek bed runs between you and Jupiter Temple, winding around to the east of Rama Shrine before passing out of sight. Behind Jupiter and Juno Temples you can see the black of Lava Butte and Chuar Lava Hill. North of them is Temple Butte. Beyond it all are the walls of the South Rim.

After Cape Final, the trail narrows again but remains easy to follow. Along the way it passes a number of other outlooks to the left. The trail ultimately peters out at a southern outlook from which you can see Freya Castle off to the right.

Camping

The Backcountry Office only gives out one camping permit to Cape Final per night, so if you have one you will be alone. Camping there is a true pleasure. Sitting at Cape Final for a sunset, watching the shadows grow long and the lights blink on atop the South Rim, is an experience that's hard to match. There are no official tent sites, so it is up to you to choose one. The bumpy rocks along the ridges make for an uncomfortable choice, but most of the woods are flat and sheltered from the wind. Watch out for cacti (the smaller ones are often hidden). Because there are no water sources, you will need to bring your own water for cooking and drinking. Keep in mind that it can get chilly at Cape Final, even in July. If you go, make sure you bring some warm clothes. While you're there, be sure to bag and hang your food, dishes and toothpaste where animals can't get to them.

7 Widforss Point Trail

SUMMARY

The Widforss Trail takes you deep into the forests of the Widforss peninsula, ending with a fine view into Grand Canyon. For lovers of wildflowers and woodland scenery, it has few rivals on the North Rim. The trail can be done as a day or overnight trip.

★ *Highly Recommended*

TRAIL INFORMATION	WIDFORSS POINT TRAIL
DISTANCE 10 miles round-trip	**DIFFICULTY** Easy
APPROXIMATE HIKING TIME 6 hours	
TRAIL CONDITION Good, unmaintained	
WATER AVAILABILITY No water	
ELEVATION CHANGE 400 feet	

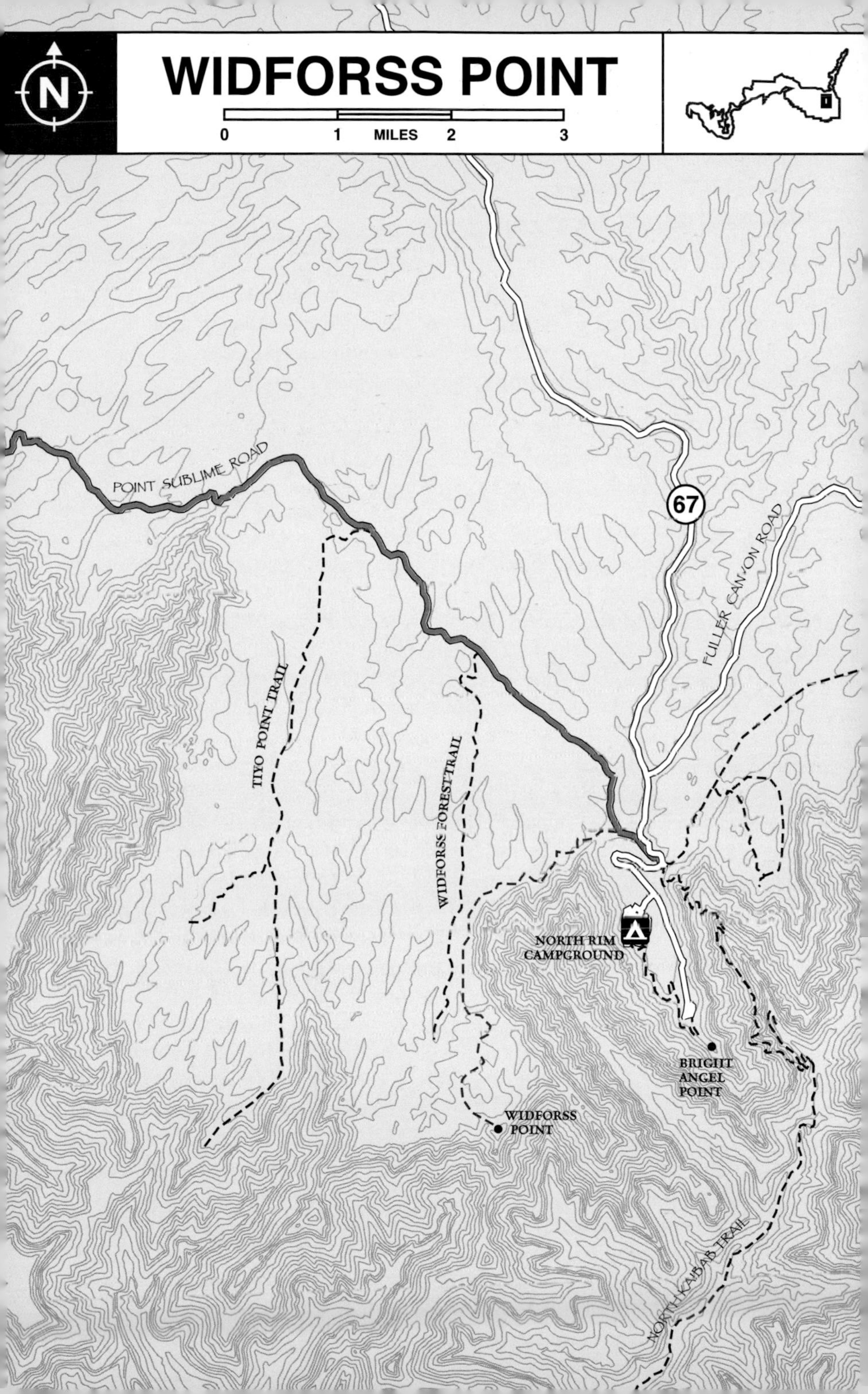

WIDFORSS POINT
N
0
1
MILES
2
3
POINT SUBLIME ROAD
67
FULLER CANYON ROAD
TIYO POINT TRAIL
WIDFORSS FOREST TRAIL
NORTH RIM CAMPGROUND
BRIGHT ANGEL POINT
WIDFORSS POINT
NORTH KAIBAB TRAIL

7 Widforss Point Trail

PARKING

There is a parking area next to the trailhead.

TRAILHEAD

From Grand Canyon Lodge, drive north on AZ-67 for about 2.5 miles until you see a sign for the turnoff to Widforss Point. Turn left onto the curving dirt road and follow it for about a half mile. There is a signed parking area for the Widforss Trail on the left. The trail leaves the south side of the parking lot.

NOTES

A small dispenser offers pamphlets for a self-guided nature walk over the first two miles of the trail. They cost a quarter (on the honor system) and are worth it.

TRAIL DESCRIPTION

From the trailhead the trail swings uphill with a small ponderosa valley below you to the left. In this stretch it feels as if you are in the Rockies, climbing cool piney mountains. You come back to Arizona when the trail reaches the rim, providing you with your first views into the Transept. The trail switches back from here and descends into the woods a short distance before climbing back to the rim. This pattern continues for the next two miles, with the trail following the rim for the most part but regularly dipping back into the trees.

You'll see several numbered wooden pegs in the ground for the first half of the trail. These pegs, marking points of interest, are deciphered by the numbers in the pamphlet available at the trailhead. Notable among them are 9 (petrified reptile tracks) and 10 (a gigantic old-growth ponderosa pine, perhaps 500 years old).

The trail along the rim has several side trails to viewpoints on the left. These are fairly similar but worth checking out. Many of the side trails lead back around to the main trail and are nice places to enjoy a break looking out into the Transept. Two and a half miles from the start, the trail swings south and leaves the rim to run through the woods. The rest of the path runs through the familiar North Rim landscape of evergreens and aspens interspersed with fire burned trunks. Between lightning and forest fires the trees of the North Rim have burned many times. A few sections of the forest are almost entirely burnt trees. The ground is pitted with holes, some of them still containing black stumpy remnants of the trees that once grew here, but there are many wildflowers as well. Beds of purple lupines blanket the ground beneath the trees, with desert paintbrushes springing up around them.

The trail runs on to the south, bending through the trees. For the most part it's flat with a few mild ups and downs. At length you begin to see the horizon through the trees, and the trail narrows as it reaches the end. There is a picnic table and some clear spaces that make for good tent sites near the end of the trail. The viewpoint is a short distance farther along the trail on a rock ledge to the right. The trail itself turns left and circles back around the campsite to form a quarter-mile loop.

8 Powell Plateau Trail

SUMMARY
Powell Plateau, a broad shoulder of land to the west of the North Rim, provides one of the most remote and rewarding day hikes in the canyon. The trail takes you into a secluded woodland amid sweeping views of Grand Canyon.

★ *Recommended*

TRAIL INFORMATION	POWELL PLATEAU TRAIL
DISTANCE 6–12 miles round-trip	**DIFFICULTY** Moderate
APPROXIMATE HIKING TIME 3–5 hours	
TRAIL CONDITION Fair, unmaintained	
WATER AVAILABILITY No water	
ELEVATION CHANGE 1,700 feet	

POWELL PLATEAU

8 Powell Plateau

PARKING

There is a parking area near the trailhead.

TRAILHEAD

Getting to the Powell Plateau trailhead isn't easy. The roads that lead there, particularly the last eight miles, are quite poor, and four-wheel drive is required. The roads referred to here are all dirt forest roads, and their numbers should be indicated at intersections by wooden stakes. From Grand Canyon Lodge, drive north on AZ-67. Four miles past the park entrance station, turn left (west) onto Forest Road 22 (a mile south of Kaibab Lodge). Drive 2.1 miles and turn left on 270 at a four-way intersection. Drive 2.3 miles and turn right on 223. Drive 5.8 miles and take a hard left on 268. After 0.3 miles bear left on 268 B and drive nine miles.

The first 1.2 miles on 268 B aren't much worse than the bumpy roads you've been driving on, but the next 7.8 miles are very bad and require a sturdy vehicle. Continue straight on this road until you come to a wider space to park in. There's a wonderful view of Muav Canyon to the left and a tentsite nearby. Although the road continues for another quarter mile, it's not worth driving. The road ends at Swamp Point, the official trailhead. There's a large water container here (used to fight forest fires) and an informative NPS sign for the trailhead is straight ahead.

NOTES

Although the Powell Plateau trail is short, a longer backpack to fully explore the area is also a good option provided you carry in enough water.

TRAIL DESCRIPTION

For the first three-quarters of a mile down to the Muav Saddle (900 feet of descent) you are on the North Bass Trail, which shares the same trailhead as the Powell Plateau Trail. The uneven and rocky trail descends a little to the left, passing through scrub oak and pines on a long traverse around a shoulder of land. Saddle Canyon and Steamboat Mountain are spread out below you to the right. After descending gently for a third of a mile, the trail switches back to the left for an even longer traverse back towards Muav Canyon. From here you can see the trail running up the side of Powell Plateau. After a half mile you descend abruptly on a series of fairly steep switchbacks. Soon you will reach the trees of Muav Saddle. The trail is a little overgrown, but not terribly difficult.

There is a four-way intersection at Muav Saddle. The North Bass Trail drops down to the left on its way to the Colorado River, and a short spur trail to Muav Cabin goes off to the right. The cabin was formerly used by the Park Service and is available for hikers to stay in overnight. The Powell Plateau Trail continues on and soon begins to climb the Plateau. Shortly past the saddle the trail swings left (uphill) and the trail becomes very overgrown. After walking through some large

pines the trail cuts left, working along the side of a wash before curving right at the wash's center. It traverses in this direction for a quarter mile and then switches back and forth as it ascends the plateau.

After a half mile of climbing, the plateau evens out and the trail becomes straighter and gentler in grade. It passes through thorny scrubland toward the trees on the flat summit of the plateau. For the next three quarters of a mile the trail is flat, winding through open ponderosa woods full of gigantic trees. The trail nears the rim twice, and the view of the main canyon is fantastic. At times, especially toward the end, the trail is faint and difficult to make out. It ends abruptly near the start of Dutton Canyon. On the rim to your left, the rocky ledges make for a great resting spot with spectacular views.

Bushwhacking through the flat, open forest of Powell Plateau can be very rewarding, as long as you have a good map and are experienced in such endeavors. Six miles from the trailhead is Dutton Point, supposedly John Wesley Powell's favorite viewpoint in Grand Canyon. Work your way along the rim to get there. You may come across some Ancestral Puebloan ruins in the course of your wanderings; hundreds of Ancestral Puebloans lived at this spot around in the 11th century, and there are over 80 Ancestral Puebloan sites recorded on Powell Plateau.

8 North Kaibab Trail

SUMMARY

The North Kaibab Trail is the only maintained trail on the North Rim that reaches the Colorado River. From start to finish, the trail passes through more geological and ecological zones than any other trail in the Canyon. Although strenuous, it's a beautiful path with modern facilities.

★ *Recommended*

TRAIL INFORMATION	NORTH KAIBAB TRAIL

DISTANCE 28 miles round-trip **DIFFICULTY** Strenuous

APPROXIMATE HIKING TIME 3–4 days

TRAIL CONDITION Excellent, maintained

WATER AVAILABILITY Piped in water available

ELEVATION CHANGE 5,855 feet

N. KAIBAB TRAIL

9 North Kaibab Trail

Day Hikes
Coconino Overlook: 1.5 miles round-trip
Supai Tunnel: 4 miles round-trip
Roaring Springs: 9.4 miles round-trip

PARKING
There is a parking lot next to the trailhead. During peak season, the lot often fills up early, but a daily shuttle runs between the parking lot and the Grand Canyon Lodge (inquire at the lodge for details).

TRAILHEAD
The North Kaibab trailhead is located two miles north of Grand Canyon Lodge on the east side of AZ-67. To get to the start of the trail, head toward the mule pens at the top of the parking lot and take a hard right down the broad, sandy trail hemmed in by two rows of logs.

NOTES
Mule trains are common on the North Kaibab Trail. If you see a mule train approaching, move to the inside of the trail and obey instructions from the mule wrangler. The steepest section of the North Kaibab Trail lies between the trailhead and Roaring Springs, dropping 3,600 feet in 4.7 miles. If you are hiking the entire trail, two days each way is recommended. Backpackers are restricted to staying in developed campgrounds. There are two campgrounds on the trail: Cottonwood (6.9 miles) and Bright Angel (14.4 miles). Piped water is available at Supai Tunnel (1.8 miles), Roaring Springs, Cottonwood Campground, and Bright Angel Campground. Bright Angel Creek is a perennial water supply, but must be treated before drinking. The water at Supai Tunnel and Roaring Springs is usually turned off in early October. The water at Cottonwood is usually left on until Thanksgiving.

TRAIL DESCRIPTION
From the trailhead, the North Kaibab Trail slopes down a gentle grade through a forest of ponderosa pine, white fir, Douglas fir, and quaking aspen. Soon the trail reaches a series of switchbacks. About a mile from the top, Coconino Overlook opens out over Roaring Spring Canyon.

From the overlook, the trail descends on switchbacks through Roaring Spring Canyon. Eventually, at 1.8 miles, you reach Supai Tunnel. A seasonal water faucet and three toilet stalls are located shortly before the entrance.

Supai Tunnel is a worthwhile destination for a day hike. The tunnel is about 20 feet long and tall enough for a mule with a rider. Once through the tunnel, you are treated to a fine view of imposing cliffs (above you to the right) streaked pink, yellow, and blue—looking more like modern art than rock walls.

On the other side of Supai Tunnel, the vegetation becomes typical of the

pinyon-juniper life zone. As you drop into the heart of Roaring Springs Canyon, the trail becomes a little less sandy and the switchbacks become more intense. The trail works along a wide ledge on the eastern side of the gorge before reaching Redwall Bridge, which takes you to the western side of the canyon. The trail climbs briefly before leveling out to a mild descent. The ledge works its way around the dramatic curves in the cliffs, with Roaring Canyon plunging away from the trail's edge. Soon, a striking rocky spire called the "Needle" rises to the left of the trail.

The trail winds along the western wall of the canyon, with some switchbacks along particularly sheer sections. As you approach Roaring Springs, you'll be able to see a cascading waterfall bursting forth from the rock on the far side of the canyon. Soon you'll reach a signed junction with a side trail leading to Roaring Springs. Roaring Springs is a scenic place filled with cottonwoods and greenery. The side trail that leads there is about a quarter of a mile long with an elevation loss of roughly 100 feet. There is a bathroom nearby and a faucet with drinking water.

As the main trail continues past the Roaring Springs junction, it passes the residence of the Roaring Springs pumphouse operator before crossing a bridge that spans Bright Angel Creek. The trail is now entering the Lower Sonoran Desert Zone, and plants such as yucca and Engelmann prickly pear cactus start to appear. The trail follows the eastern side of Bright Angel Canyon for 1.4 miles, undulating up and down mildly before reaching Cottonwood Campground.

Cottonwood is a pleasant place—not quite as shady as the name implies, but cooler than the rest of the desert. Toilets and drinking water are available from May through October. Campsites include a picnic table, two metal boxes for food storage, and a T-bar you can use to hang packs or laundry from (the T-bar used to be used for hanging food, but local critters have figured out how to climb the smooth metal pole). Cottonwood's views of Oza Butte and Bright Angel Point are impressive. At night, you can often see the lights of Grand Canyon Lodge.

Past the campground the trail continues to follow the eastern side of Bight Angel Creek. About a half mile from the campground the trail crosses Wall Creek, and after another half mile you'll reach the side trail to Ribbon Falls. Ribbon falls is one of the most popular sights on the North Kaibab Trail. The side trail leading there is a quarter mile long. It crosses over a small bridge, runs along a stream, and clambers over some rocks before opening up onto a hidden grotto with a 100-foot waterfall. Ribbon Falls was named by early surveyor François Matthes, who thought the water from the falls resembled ribbons blowing in the breeze. The top of the falls spills about 40 feet onto a moss covered travertine cone. Maidenhair fern, golden columbine, and scarlet monkeyflower thrive here. There's a trail to the left that takes you above the moss and behind the falls. Another trail leads up to a rocky alcove far to the right. (Be careful on both of these trails, the drop-off is steep and the trails can get slippery.) With its tranquil atmosphere and cooling sprays, Ribbon Falls is an excellent place to spend a hot summer afternoon if you're hiking between Bright Angel Campground and Cottonwood Campground. (Note: Although there is another trail leading back to the North Kaibab Trail from the Ribbon Falls, it can get tricky and is best avoided.)

Ribbon Falls

From the Ribbon Falls junction, the North Kaibab Trail ascends a series of steep switchbacks for a quarter of a mile before falling back into its typical descent. The trail runs along the creek for the next mile and a half, with an unavoidable wet swampy area towards the end of this stretch.

Past the marshy swamp, the trail enters the awe inspiring four-mile corridor known as The Box. Made of 1.7 billion year-old Vishnu Schist and Zoroaster Granite, the walls of The Box tower above you as you walk between them. In places, the walls are over 1,000 feet high. As a result, much of this section is covered in shade for long periods of time. The Box has a primeval feel. Its twists and turns shut out the rest of the world, leaving behind only the sounds of rushing water and chirping birds. Bird watchers will definitely want their binoculars out here. There are four bridges that criss cross the Box, but for the most part the trail follows the eastern side. After the fourth bridge, the path spills out into a more open area, becoming a little sunnier as it heads three quarters of a mile towards Phantom Ranch.

The buildings at Phantom Ranch line the trail for half a mile, luring hikers with air conditioning and cold beer. Bright Angel Campground is located farther down the trail. Bright Angel Campground has the same amenities as Cottonwood, but is always more crowded. The tent sites are located on the right hand side of the cool and refreshing waters of Bright Angel Creek. Overheated hikers love to wade in the creek for extended periods of time, especially in the summer months when temperatures top 100 degrees. In the evening, Phantom Ranch offers ranger programs. (Note: Bright Angel Campground has many animals that have grown quite bold in their campsite expeditions. Be careful with your food and never feed the animals.)

The trail to the Colorado River is another quarter mile down the left hand side of Bright Angel Creek. You can cross the river on one of two impressive bridges. If you haven't hiked enough already, you can loop between the two bridges along the South Kaibab Trail, which features some extensive Ancestral Puebloan ruins on its north side.

For a return trip in the summer, start very early in the morning, well before sunrise if possible. It will be much cooler during this time, making the strenuous hike back much more pleasant.

BRIGHT ANGEL CREEK

Bright Angel Creek was originally named Silver Creek by John Wesley Powell on his 1869 Colorado River expedition, but he changed the name a few years later in the published account of his journey. "The little affluent which we have discovered here," he wrote, "is a clear, beautiful creek, or river, as it would be termed in this western country, where streams are not abundant. We have named one stream, away above, in honor of the great chief of the 'Bad Angels,' [Dirty Devil Creek] and as this is a beautiful contrast to that, we conclude to name it 'Bright Angel.'"

Bright Angel Creek

10 Thunder River Trail

SUMMARY

The Thunder River Trail is a challenging, multi-day route that descends nearly 6,000 feet to the Colorado River. The scenery is spectacular, but due to the trail's steep scrambles, river crossings, and isolation it should only be attempted by experienced backpackers. The Deer Creek Trail, an offshoot of Thunder River Trail, is perhaps even more impressive than the Thunder River Trail itself.

★ *Highly Recommended*

TRAIL INFORMATION | **THUNDER RIVER TRAIL**

DISTANCE 24–30 miles round-trip **DIFFICULTY** Very Strenuous

APPROXIMATE HIKING TIME 3–4 days

TRAIL CONDITION Fair, unmaintained

WATER AVAILABILITY Thunder River, Deer Creek

ELEVATION CHANGE 6,650 feet

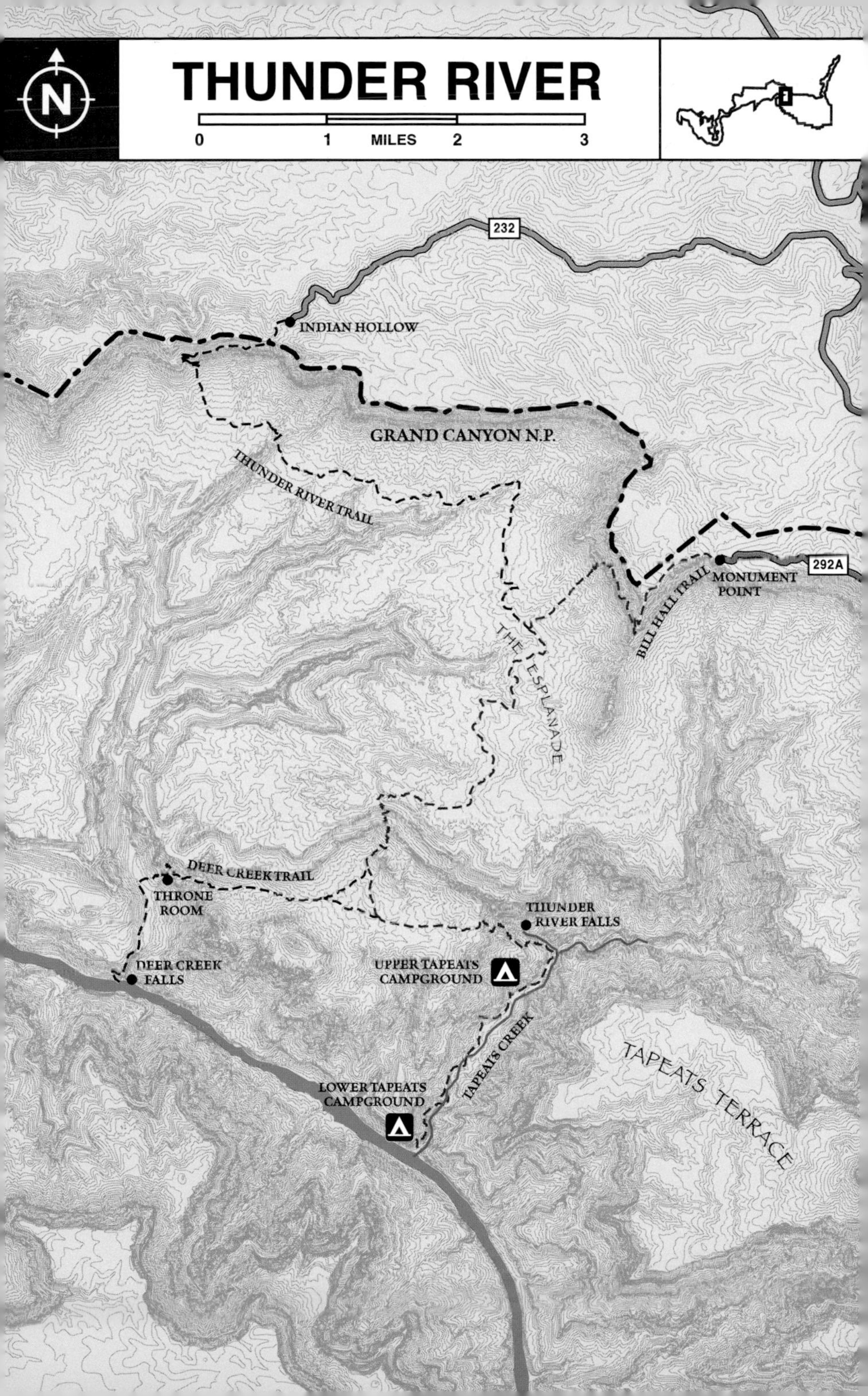
THUNDER RIVER
N
0
1
MILES
2
3
232
INDIAN HOLLOW
GRAND CANYON N.P.
THUNDER RIVER TRAIL
THE ESPLANADE
BILL HALL TRAIL
MONUMENT POINT
292A
DEER CREEK TRAIL
THRONE ROOM
THUNDER RIVER FALLS
DEER CREEK FALLS
UPPER TAPEATS CAMPGROUND
TAPEATS CREEK
LOWER TAPEATS CAMPGROUND
TAPEATS TERRACE

10 Thunder River Trail

PARKING

There is a parking area next to the trailhead.

TRAILHEAD

The first challenge of the Thunder River Trail is getting there. The trailhead at Monument Point is at the end of a confusing network of forest roads. From Grand Canyon Lodge, drive north on AZ-67. Four miles past the park entrance station, turn left (west) onto Forest Road 22 (1 mile south of Kaibab Lodge). Although the roads are dirt from this point on, most cars should be able to handle them. Drive 11 miles on road 22, passing Dry Park fire tower. When you come to a T intersection, turn left onto road 206. Drive 6 miles and take a right onto road 214. Drive 3 miles and bear right on to road 272. Drive 6 miles and turn right at the T intersection onto road 292. There will be a sign to go straight 2 miles for Monument Point. Go straight, then turn onto road 292A. Drive 4 miles to the Bill Hall trailhead, a large open space with a gate at the end. Although it begins at 7000 feet (as opposed to 6250 for the Thunder River Trailhead), the Bill Hall Trail takes five miles off of your trip to Surprise Valley or Tapeats Creek. It is recommended if you're going to Tapeats Creek or the Colorado River.

NOTES

There is no water between Monument Point and Thunder River. If you're backpacking you'll want to cache a few gallons on the Esplanade for the return trip. Camping at large is legal anywhere between the trailhead and about 1.5 miles north of Upper Tapeats campsite. In the summer, the trail is sometimes closed due to extreme heat. If you are here in the summer, carry extra water and bring a water filter or iodine to safely replenish your water supply.

TRAIL DESCRIPTION

After hiking through the trailhead gate, pass the forest road to your right and turn left by the NPS information sign. The trail immediately climbs through a scorched landscape of burned out trees—the result of a 1996 wildfire touched off by lightning. The trail follows the rim for three quarters of a mile, passing several fine viewpoints along the way. Soon the trail splits, with one branch heading left to a viewpoint and the other continuing to the right. Both branches rejoin not long after the fork.

The trail eventually crests a hill and continues, quite flat, for another three quarters of a mile. A cairn marks the spot near the tip of Monument Point where the trail leaves the rim behind and dives down into the canyon. At this point the trail becomes crumbly and challenging. Careful footing is a must. The trail switches back and forth a few times down the steep, rocky slope. After descending a few hundred feet, the trail veers right as it traverses the slope. As it wraps around

the ridge, the beautiful expanse of red slickrock known as the Esplanade spreads out below you. Along the traverse there are several sections of alarming exposure to steep cliffs. When you finally reach the end of the traverse, there will be a relatively difficult descent/scramble of about 10 feet. If your packs are heavy you may want to ferry them down before descending yourself. (A short rope to lower your packs can be handy here.)

At the end of the traverse is a mile-long stretch of switchbacks through pinyon-juniper woodlands. Although quite steep at first, the slope of the land becomes gentler and gentler as you drop towards the Esplanade. The trail then runs at a fairly smooth grade through scrub and sagebrush terrain before intersecting the Thunder River Trail. There is a small sign in the ground indicating that the Indian Hollow Trailhead is to your right and Thunder River is to your left. Bear left at the junction and head southeast.

The next 2.5 miles of the trail passes through the Esplanade and is well marked by small cairns. For the most part the trail is very easy to follow, although there may be moments of uncertainty. Pay close attention to where you're going. As the Esplanade slopes down, the trail picks its way through several unique rock formations with panoramic views unfolding below.

Soon, you'll reach the southern rim of the Esplanade. At this point the trail descends, switching back and forth along a steep rocky slope. The footing is uneven in places, but sturdy rock walls guard the sides of the trail. The trail's descent continues for about a mile and a half until you reach Surprise Valley.

The trail through Surprise Valley is flat and clear as it winds through the desert scrub. After approximately one mile the Deer Creek Trail veers off to the

right (there's no sign, only a split in the dirt paths). Take the left fork to get to Thunder River. After another mile, you'll be able to hear the waterfall that marks the start of Thunder River. The path then descends 1,500 feet in a steady stream of switchbacks. Half a mile down, there's a short side trail that leads to the edge of the waterfall.

The waterfall is a sight to behold. Bursting forth from a limestone cave, it cascades down the parched terrain and supports a dense corridor of lush vegetation on both sides—cottonwoods, maidenhair fern, and monkeyflower thrive here. On a hot summer day, the spray near the falls is fantastically refreshing.

After the waterfall, the main trail continues down a series of switchbacks to the confluence of Thunder River and Tapeats Creek. Soon, the trail passes through Upper Tapeats campsite.

Past the campsite, the trail consists of a series of exposed ledge walks, bushwhacks through thorny vegetation, and tricky river crossings. Depending on the spring runoff, Tapeats creek can be extremely hazardous—in a heavy snow year it can be almost impossible to cross the river due to high water. Do not take this trail unless you have plenty of time and the necessary expertise to safely navigate through such unfriendly terrain. The challenge can be fun, but it is a real challenge. After the last stream crossing, the path climbs gradually to a high side canyon rim hundreds of feet above the water. The trail is good here and the view of the creek emptying into the Colorado is impressive. The sandy beach that makes up Lower Tapeats is a peaceful, isolated oasis among steep canyon walls.

Thunder River Falls

10 Deer Creek Narrows

DEER CREEK NARROWS

The Deer Creek Trail is a spectacular six-mile round-trip offshoot of the Thunder River Trail. It starts at the junction with the Thunder River Trail in Surprise Valley (see preceding trail description). After the junction, the trail descends until it reaches a large jumble of gray rocks with views of Deer Creek in the valley below. The trail then traverses a ledge to the right, swings around to the left, and drops down to a secluded waterfall bursting forth through the Muav Limestone. A small trail leads to an open space behind the falls.

On the other side of the waterfall is a shaded alcove known as the Throne Room. Scattered throughout this open space are large slabs of rocks that have been arranged into surprisingly comfortable throne-like seats.

After leaving the Throne Room, the trail continues its descent until it reaches Deer Creek. After crossing the creek (the best crossing is a little to the left of where the trail hits the water), the trail continues along the southern bank, passing through giant reed grass and over some scattered rocks. Soon the creek tumbles down into beautiful Deer Creek Narrows. The trail runs at the same level as Deer Creek a short distance before plunging into Deer Creek Narrows. The serpentine rock walls of Deer Creek Narrows have been gracefully carved out of Tapeats Sandstone, twisting up and around you with the creek rushing below. Along the walls next to the trail are handprints painted on by the Indians that used to inhabit this part of Grand Canyon. They were created by blowing white pigment around a flat hand placed against the wall, most likely with a hollow reed or piece of bone. Enjoy, but do not touch.

The path follows the right hand side of the creek, and is very safe in all but a few places. After passing through Deer Creek Narrows, the trail reaches a stunning overlook high above the Colorado River. From here the trail turns right and works its way down to the river. After switching back and forth, the trail emerges near the river. There is some poison ivy here, so be careful.

Deer Creek emerges from Deer Creek Narrows in a spectacular hundred-foot waterfall that comes crashing down from the slot canyon above. Deer Creek Falls is the largest waterfall visible from the Colorado River in the Grand Canyon. Alongside the falls is a shallow but refreshing swimming hole. This area is extremely popular with river trips in the summer. The misty wind of the falls stings as you approach it and the roar of the water crashing down is deafening. A rainbow often appears in the mist surrounding the base of Deer Creek Falls, creating a spectacular finale to a long day trekking across Surprise Valley.

Throne Room Waterfall

Deer Creek Narrows

Loop Walk

For those who don't wish to retrace their steps back up Deer Creek, there is an unofficial, unnamed trail back along the Colorado to Lower Tapeats. The trail is about four miles long, and it's not recommended for anyone without good route-finding skills. To get there, return to the start of the narrows, cross them before the creek drops below the trail, and climb the scrubby slope ahead of you. When you reach the saddle, you'll be able to see the faint dirt trail snaking away on the other side. The path is fairly clear and consistent, running a few hundred feet above the River for about two miles before dropping down to the Colorado. The higher part of the path from Deer Creek towards Tapeats Creek is among the wildest, grandest, and most isolated routes north of the river. When in doubt, stay high—the descent to the river is very clear. The trail continues along the rocky beach, marked erratically by cairns. Take care during this section, as the path grows fainter. There are a few simple scrambles on the way. After another two miles you will get to Tapeats Creek. It's the next big stream entering the Colorado after Deer Creek and is difficult to mistake. From Lower Tapeats Creek take the Thunder River Trail back to the campsite.

Deer Creek Falls

HAVASU CANYON

☆ ☆ ☆ ☆ ☆

Havasu Falls

HAVASU CANYON

TO GRAND CANYON visitors in the know, the name Havasu conjures up images of a remote desert paradise. This deep side canyon, located about 35 miles west of Grand Canyon Village, is one of the most shockingly beautiful places in the Southwest. For over 700 years Havasu Canyon has been the home of the Havasupai Indians, the "People of the Blue-Green Water," who derive their name from the vivid turquoise stream that flows through center of the canyon. The Havasupai Indians continue to live in the tiny village of Supai (pop. 400) located 2,000 feet below the rim. A short distance from the village are Havasu Falls and Mooney Falls, two of the most gorgeous waterfalls in North America.

Although Havasu Canyon only receives nine inches of rain a year, it drains a 3,000 square-mile basin, enough to create a steady stream flowing through the canyon at about 38 million gallons a day. Even more impressive, the stream tumbles down the canyon in a series of beautiful pools and waterfalls. The color of the water, an unearthly blue more typical of the Caribbean than the desert Southwest, is caused by a light coating of travertine (calcium carbonate) that reflects off the riverbed.

Is Havasu Canyon too good to be true? Almost. Due to its rugged, remote location, getting here is a bit of a challenge, requiring long drives along desolate roads and a rugged descent into the canyon by a) foot, b) mule, or c) helicopter. No roads lead to Supai, which is the last town in the United States where daily mail is still delivered by mule. Furthermore, all visitors to Havasu must obtain a permit before entering the canyon. To prevent overcrowding, the Havasupai keep the number of permits issued deliberately low at about 35,000 per year.

In many ways, Havasu Canyon feels like the land that time forgot. The roughly 400 Havasupai Indians still living in Supai continue to speak their native tongue, horses and dogs freely roam the dirt roads, and illumination is only provided by the sun. All this, combined with breathtaking natural scenery, makes a visit to Havasu Canyon one of the most remarkable adventures in America.

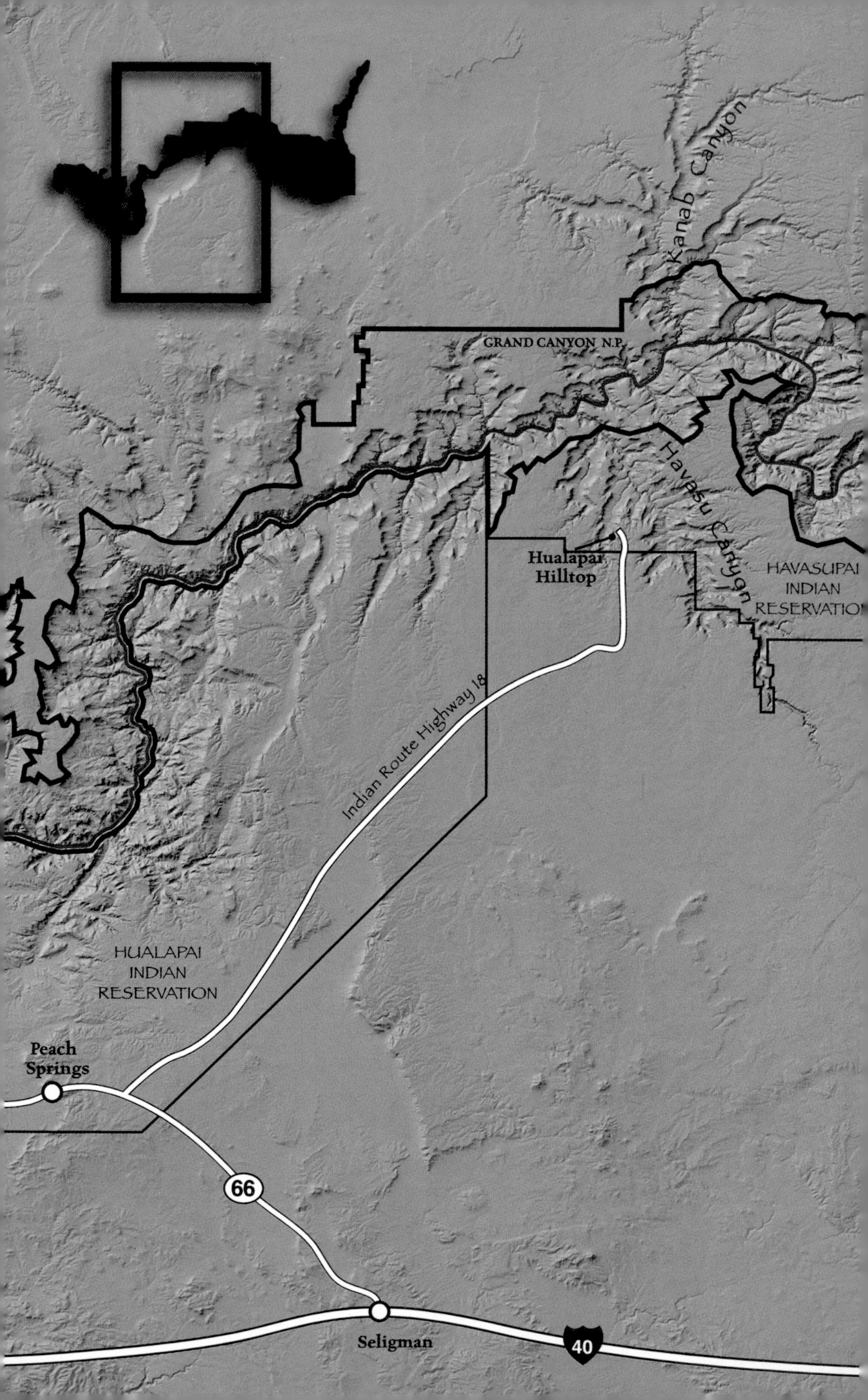
Kanab Canyon
GRAND CANYON N.P.
Havasu Canyon
Hualapai
Hilltop
HAVASUPAI
INDIAN
RESERVATIO
Indian Route Highway 18
HUALAPAI
INDIAN
RESERVATION
Peach
Springs
66
Seligman
40

HAVASU CANYON
N
0
1
MILES
2
3
UKWALLA POINT
MOONEY FALLS
3
HAVASU FALLS
2
WATAHOMIGI POINT
1
SUPAI
MANAKACHA POINT
HAVASU CANYON
LONG MESA
HUALAPAI CANYON
HUALAPAI HILLTOP

Havasu Canyon BASICS

BASIC INFO

For general info about Havasu Canyon, check out the Havasupai Tribe's web site at www.havasupaitribe.com

GETTING TO HAVASU

Although Havasu Canyon only lies about 35 miles west of Grand Canyon Village, it's about 200 miles away by road. The trail to the village of Supai starts at the rim of Havasu Canyon at a spot called Hualapai Hilltop. To get there from Grand Canyon Village, take I-40 to the town of Seligman and turn onto AZ-66 heading toward Peach Springs. A little under 30 miles past Seligman (six miles east of Peach Springs) turn onto Indian Route Highway 18 and follow it 56 miles to Hualapai Hilltop. From the hilltop you have three options to get to Supai:

On Foot—The trail to Supai is about eight miles. Plan on roughly three hours hiking down and four hours hiking up. Despite a series of strenuous switchbacks near the top, the majority of the trail is a moderate/easy hike. To lighten your load, you can arrange to have your bag carried down by mule.

By Mule—Mule rides to Supai cost $70 per person one-way, $120 round-trip. They are best booked through the lodge (928-448-2111). A ride to the campground, located past the village, can be arranged by Havasupai Tourist Enterprises (928-448-2121) for $75 one-way, $150 round-trip. One mule can also carry up to four bags for the price of one rider.

By Helicopter—Skydance Helicopters (800-882-1651) runs trips between Hualapai Hilltop and Supai. Cost: $70 each way. Papillon Helicopters (928-638-2419) also runs one-day excursions (including a horse ride to the waterfalls) from Grand Canyon Airport in Tusayan for $450 round-trip.

PERMITS & FEES

All visitors *must* have an advance reservation at either the campground or lodge prior to arrival. There's also a $20 entrance fee. If you're staying at the lodge, the fee is added to your bill. Campers should pay the fee at the tourist office in Supai.

LODGING

A small, two-story lodge in Supai offers motel-style rooms that sleep up to four. All rooms have air conditioning and private bathrooms, but no telephones or TV. Between May and October the lodge is generally booked months in advance. **Rates**: $125 (928-448-2111).

CAMPING

A gorgeous 200-person campground, located two miles beyond Supai near Havasu Falls, is open year-round. Campsites are located on either side of Havasu Stream, but no fires are permitted. Reservations (928-448-2141) are usually easy to come except during peak summer season or on busy holiday weekends. Cost: $10 per person. (On a more macabre note: the campground is located on the Havasupai's ancient burial grounds. In the late 1800s Congress seized much of Havasu Canyon, including the burial grounds, which was later dug up and mined for lead, silver and zinc. The lands were ultimately returned to the Havasupai in 1975.)

FOOD & DINING

Supai only has one restaurant: the Tribal Cafe, which serves cafeteria-style food near Supai Lodge. Hours vary, but the cafe is generally open 6 a.m.–6 p.m. in the summer, 8 a.m.–5 p.m. in the winter (928-448-2981, cash only). There's also a small grocery store across from the Cafe that sells basic goods at steep prices.

LODGING NEAR HUALAPAI HILLTOP

Driving to Hualapai Hilltop from Grand Canyon Village or any major city takes several hours, and after a grueling drive the last thing you'll want to do is start another grueling trip down Havasu Canyon. A better option is to spend the night at one of the handful of hotels located along AZ-66, which, although at least an hour away from Hualapai Hilltop, will make for a much less stressful trip.

HUALAPAI LODGE

A modern, sixty-room hotel located in Peach Springs Rates: $90–$130. (888-255-9550, www.grandcanyonresort.com).

GRAND CANYON CAVERNS INN

This 48-room motel is located next to Grand Canyon Cavern, a natural limestone cavern 210 feet underground. Rates: $65–$75 (877-422-4459, www.gccaverns.com).

1 Supai Village

In the 1930s an anthropologist visiting Supai remarked that it was, "the only spot in the United States where native culture has remained in anything like its pristine condition." Although modernization has since come to Supai in the form of electricity, telephones and the Internet, the pace of life remains distinctly different from that of the outside world—and the Havasupai like it that way. Any suggestions of building a road into the canyon have always been rejected.

The earliest residents of Havasu Canyon were an ancient culture called the Cohonina. It's unknown if the Havasupai are descendents of the Cohonina, or if they are an entirely separate group, but by A.D. 1300 the Havasupai had established themselves in Havasu canyon. They took advantage of the steady flow of water in the summer, and moved above the rim in the winter when the tall walls of Havasu Canyon only let in about five hours of sunlight in per day.

In 1776 a Spanish missionary named Francisco Thomás Garcés became the first white man to set eyes on Havasu Canyon. Several decades later, American prospectors arrived in the canyon in search of gold. But these disturbances were only temporary. Then, in 1866, Congress granted much of the Havasupai's traditional lands to the Atlantic and Pacific Railroad, and the Havasupai were forced onto a reservation in Havasu Canyon less than one square mile in size. Finally in 1975, after much legal wrangling, the Havasupai Reservation was expanded to its present size of 185,000 acres.

2 Havasu Falls

This waterfall, Havasu Canyon's star attraction, is located about two miles past the village of Supai. To get there, follow Supai's main road down the canyon until it turns into a dirt path. After a mile and a half you'll reach Navajo Falls, a steep series of cascades tumbling down an overgrown cliff. Continue following the path for about half a mile to reach Havasu Falls. As the trail starts to descend along the western canyon wall, Havasu Falls makes a sudden, spectacular appearance to your right. At this point you're at eye level with the top of the 100-foot falls. Continue down the trail to reach several well-troden side trails that lead to a beach area. Although crowded in the summer, this beach is without question one of the most spectacular swimming holes in America.

A century ago Havasu Falls was a much different waterfall than the one you see today. Back then the waterfall cascaded over of the cliff in a wide curtain of water. Then, several decades ago, a flash flood roared through Havasu Canyon and knocked out a large notch in the cliff. Suddenly, the creek was channeled into a much narrower—and much more spectacular—waterfall. Other flash floods, however, have been much less kind. A flash flood in 1993 destroyed several beautiful travertine terraces at the base of the falls that formed a series of cascading pools. Today, brand new terraces are slowly rebuilding.

Note: Because Havasu Canyon drains such a vast area, flash floods are a constant threat. See page 23 for more on flash floods.

3 Mooney Falls

Mooney Falls is the tallest waterfall in Havasu Canyon. At 196 feet, it's taller than Niagara Falls. To get there, follow the main path one mile past Havasu Falls to a stunning overlook. To reach the base of the falls, however, you'll have to descend a series of slippery ladders and steps that are not for the faint of heart. Use caution if you follow this route. Although the trail continues past the base of Mooney Falls, it becomes quite rugged as it descends farther down the canyon.

The Havasupai call Mooney Falls "Mother of the Waters", and they consider it to be their most sacred waterfall. The name Mooney Falls comes from a tragic accident that occurred here in 1880. In that year, a group of American prospectors descended Havasu Canyon in the hopes of finding gold, but when they reached this waterfall they could go no farther. Several Havasupai Indians who accompanied the prospectors told them that no man had ever passed beyond the waterfall, only the "birds of the air or spirits of the dead." Undeterred, a man named Daniel Mooney asked to be lowered down by rope. With a rope tied around his waist, a group of miners and Havasupai lowered him over the falls. But during his descent the rope became stuck in a jagged crevice, and as the men struggled to free the rope it began to fray. Suddenly the rope snapped, and Mooney fell to his death. Unable to reach their friend, the remaining prospectors were forced to return 10 months later and build a ladder to the base of the falls. By the time they reached his body, it was encrusted in a fresh layer of travertine, and he was buried where he lay.